MANAGING LYRIC STRUCTURE

by

PAT PATTISON

BERKLEE COLLEGE OF MUSIC

Berklee Press
Publications

Distributed by

Hal Leonard Publishing Corporation

7777 West Bluemound Road P.O. Box 13819 Milwaukee, WI 53213

BERKLEE PRESS, BOSTON 02215.

MANAGING LYRIC STRUCTURE

CONTENTS

FOREWORD   *vii*

PERMISSION AND ACKNOWLEDGMENTS   *viii*

INTRODUCTION   1

CHAPTER ONE
NUMBER OF PHRASES: GETTING YOUR BALANCE   3
   Lyric Phrases/Musical Phrases   4
   Balancing/Unbalancing   5
   Spotlighting Important Ideas   6
   Moving One Section Forward into Another   7
   Contrasting One Section with Another   8

CHAPTER TWO
LENGTH OF PHRASES: CONTROLLING YOUR SPEED   11
   Contrasting Sections   15

CHAPTER THREE
RHYTHM: SETTING UP, SHUTTING DOWN   19
   Syllables   19
   Patterns   23
   Rhythm   25
   Paradigm One   28
   Structural Pentad   28
   Paradigm Two   30
   Deceptive Closure   31
   Paradigm Three   31
   Unexpected Closure   32

CHAPTER FOUR
RHYME: TAKING TOTAL CONTROL   34
   Rhyme Scheme   36
   Rhyme Structure   37
   Balance   37
   Pace   39
   Flow   40
   Closure   43
   Types of Closure   45
   Rhyme Strategies   49

CHAPTER FIVE

FORM: TOSSING THE BALLS TOGETHER 53

Song Elements 53

Verse 53

Chorus 55

Song System 56

Bridge 57

Transitional Bridge 61

Refrain 63

Hook 64

Building Sections 64

Number of Phrases 66

Length of Phrases 68

Rhythm of Phrases 69

Rhyme Scheme 71

CHAPTER SIX

SONG FORMS: THE BIG SHOW 74

Verse/Refrain 74

Verse/Refrain Plus Bridge 76

Verse/Chorus 77

Verse/Chorus Plus Bridge 81

Verse/Transitional Bridge/Chorus 82

Verse/Transitional Bridge/Refrain 86

CHAPTER SEVEN

HOOK PLACEMENT AND FOCUS: TURNING THE LIGHTS ON 89

Put the Hook at the Beginning or End of Its Section 89

Keep the Structure Pointing Forward Until You Get to the Hook 92

Repeat the Hook 93

Use Sound to Spotlight the Hook 96

Use the Hook's Rhythm in Other Strategic Places 97

AFTERWORD 102

Pat Pattison has been teaching lyric writing and poetry at Berklee College of Music since 1975. He played a central role in developing Berklee's unique songwriting major, the first complete songwriting degree offered anywhere. Doctoral work in philosophy at Indiana University and a Master of Arts in Literary Criticism "... gave me wonderful tools for digging into lyrics to see what makes them work." In addition to his work for TV and film, as well as numerous clinics and workshops, Pat writes monthly articles for *Home and Studio Recording* magazine.

FOREWORD

This is not a general book in lyric writing. It has a very specific purpose: *to help you handle your lyric structures more effectively.*

You study the techniques of lyric writing for the same reason you take piano lessons: even though by trial and error you could probably catch on by yourself, it will save you time when someone shows you fingerings that have been proven to work. You get better faster, and enjoy the true creative possibilities of your instrument sooner.

If you have written lyrics before and you want to take a new look, this book will help you gain even greater control and understanding of your craft. If you have not written lyrics before, this book will start you off in a healthy direction. But be warned: this is a very focused book. Good structure is not a substitute for good writing. It is only a part of it.

Along with information on lyric structure, you will find exercises to help you make it part of your own writing. It will give you new tools and help you eliminate some of the trial and error you would normally have had to go through.

Of course, information alone will not help you unless you do something with it to make it your own. Shape it to fit your grip; learn it by practice and experience. Mix it in with your own talents.

This book will show you ways to say things better. It will help you manage timing and placement. That is the point of structure. By the time you finish, you will know more about lyric structure than you ever thought possible. It will help you be a better writer.

PERMISSIONS & ACKNOWLEDGMENTS

Many of the examples in this book are original. These are not:

"Be Still My Beating Heart," by Sting. Copyright © 1987 by Magnetic Publishing Ltd. Represented by Regatta Music/Illegal Songs. All rights reserved. Used by permission.

"Between Fathers and Sons," by John Jarvis and Gary Nicholson. Copyright © 1986 by Tree Publishing Co., Inc. and Cross Keys Publishing Co., Inc. All rights reserved. International Copyright Secured. Used by permission of the Publisher.

"Can't Fight This Feeling," Kevin Cronin. Copyright © 1984 by Fate Music, ASCAP. All rights reserved. Used by permission.

"Eighteen Wheels and a Dozen Roses," by Gene Nelson, and Paul Nelson. Copyright ©1988 by Warner-Tamerlane publishing Corp., Beleivus Or Not Music, and Screen Gems-EMI Music, Inc. All rights reserved. Used by permission.

"The Great Pretender," by Buck Ram. Copyright © 1955 by Panther Music Corp. Copyright Renewed.

"It Was a Very Good Year," by Ervin Drake. Copyright © 1965 by Chappel and Co. All rights reserved. Used by Permission.

"My Old Kentucky Home," by Randy Newman. Copyright © 1967 by January Music Corp., a division of A. Schroeder International LTD. International Copyright Secured. All rights reserved. Used by Permission.

"Slow Healing Heart," by Jim Rushing. Copyright © 1984 by Maypop Music, a division of Wildcountry, Inc. All rights reserved. Used by permission.

"Tickle Me," by Randy Newman. Copyright © 1967 by Unichappel Music, Inc. All rights reserved. Used by Permission.

"Why Can't I Have You?," by Ric Ocasek. Copyright © 1984 by Lido Music, Inc. Worldwide administration rights controlled by Lido Music, Inc. All rights reserved

"Years," by Beth Neilsen Chapman. Copyright © 1987 by Warner-Tamerlane Publishing Corp. All rights reserved. Used by Permission.

"Haitian Divorce," by Walter Becker and Donald Fagen Copyright © 1976, 1978 By Duchess Music Corporation. Rights administered by MCA Music Publishing, a division of MCA Inc. All rights reserved. Used by permission.

"Your Gold Teeth II," by Walter Becker and Donald Fagen. Copyright © 1975, 1976 by MCA Music Publishing, a division of MCA Inc. All rights reserved. Used by permission.

I co-wrote some of the original examples:

"Homecoming," with Wendy Levy.
"Skin Tight," with Ken Barken.
"Southern Comfort," with Mike Ihde and Donna Starr.
"These are the Days," with Phil Wilson.
"This Bottle and Me," with Bob Weingart.
"Teddy Doesn't Live Here Anymore," with Randy Klein.
"You Never Let Me Down," with Jimmy Kachulis.

All original examples contained herein, including those listed above, are by Pat Pattison, Copyrights © 1979–1990 by featherrain Music, PO Box 349, Boston, MA 02123. Used by permission. All rights reserved.

Thanks to Bob Weingart and Jimmy Kachulis whose many excellent suggestions and comments played a major role in the development of this book. To Jack Perricone for unwavering support. To Bob Weingart and Sky Cappeletti for diligent editing and proofing. To Susan Benjamin for suggestions, editing, proofing, and support. To my son, Jason. And deepest thanks to my students at Berklee College of Music for their enthusiasm, their insight, and their love of writing.

INTRODUCTION
LYRIC ELEMENTS: THE GREAT JUGGLING ACT

BE STILL MY BEATING HEART
It would be better to be cool
It's not time to be open just yet
A lesson just learned is so hard to forget

—Sting, "BE STILL MY BEATING HEART"

You will have no trouble learning about lyric structure. It is simple, just like juggling. When a juggler keeps four balls in the air at once it may seem like magic, but there is no magic involved. The juggler learned by throwing one ball up and catching it, throwing and catching, stopping and starting the motion; always gaining greater control over the movement of the ball. Then came two balls, then three, throwing and catching, stopping and starting, with greater and greater control.

As a lyricist, you must learn to juggle four balls.

We will start with one ball, then work slowly and carefully to two, three, and finally four balls. Start by looking at the fine verse above by Sting, and answering these questions.

1. How many phrases does it have?
2. How long is each phrase?
3. What is the rhythm of each phrase?
4. How are rhymes arranged?

Any time you write a verse (or any part of a lyric for that matter) you will have to deal with these four lyric elements.

1. How many phrases will I have?
2. How long will each phrase be?
3. What rhythms will I use in each phrase?
4. How should I arrange the rhymes?

You usually won't ask the questions before you begin to write, but you will as you write and rewrite. The more control you have over each of these lyric elements, the better you can make them work together to make the lyric go where *you* want it to go. Stopping and starting, making it move. If you practice enough you will move your words with the ease of a juggler.

CHAPTER ONE
NUMBER OF PHRASES: GETTING YOUR BALANCE

> Who are these children who scheme and run wild?
>
> Who speak with their wings and the way that they smile?
>
> What are the secrets they trace in the sky?
>
> And why do you tremble each time they ride by?
>
> —Fagen & Becker "YOUR GOLD TEETH"

The first thing to ask is "What is a phrase?" Phrases are sentences or natural pieces of sentences sometimes called "clauses." Here are some examples of phrases:

> Who are these children
>
> who scheme and run wild
>
> who speak with their wings
>
> and the way that they smile
>
> what are the secrets
>
> they trace in the sky
>
> and why do you tremble
>
> each time they ride by

As you can see, when Steely Dan (Donald Fagen & Walter Becker) wrote these lyrics, they wrote in phrases. Each of these lyric phrases also matches a musical phrase. You can see that the shorter phrases can go together easily and naturally to form longer ones.

> Who are these children who scheme and run wild?

Are the longer or shorter phrases the real ones? They both are. The difference is that sometimes smaller phrases like

> who scheme and run wild

depend on being part of something else to sound natural. But they still have an identity of their own, not like:

> who scheme and

which is not a phrase at all. It clearly needs something else.

When you write music for lyric phrases, just remember that phrases made of notes are a lot like phrases made of words. Sometimes they are made to be part of something bigger

> who scheme and run wild

and sometimes they are made to stand alone.

> Who are these children who scheme and run wild?

Even short phrases often stand alone.

> Why don't you tickle me?
>
> He shouts.
>
> She bites.

Any book on English Grammar has more than enough to say about phrases, clauses, and sentences. It is enough here to look at a few examples. For convenience, call them all "phrases." Prepositional phrases:

> *After the rain,* the birds sang madly.
>
> Starships exploded *over the shoulder of Orion.*

Verbal Phrases:

> *Soaring on paper wings* is risky business. (Gerund)
>
> *Barely cracking a smile,* he bowed. (Participle)

The next phrases contain both a subject and a verb, but still depend on being part of something bigger. Can you see why?

Adjective phrases (modify nouns):

> She longed for someone *who would serve her forever.*

Adverb phrases (modify verbs):

> *When the fog lifted,* she turned for home.

Noun phrases (used as subject, predicate, or object):

> *What you see* is a broken man. (Subject)
>
> Sex is not *what it is cracked up to be.* (Predicate)
>
> Hit the dealers *where it hurts the most.* (Object)

Each of the phrases has a word that connects it to a *part* of the main sentence. (Words like "who, what, when where, why, that.") These words turn the phrases into dependents rather that self-reliant individuals.

When you talk, you do not need a book on English Grammar. Talking comes naturally. A good little book on grammar might be a handy thing to have around. Not that you have to write proper sentences. Sometimes just for information.

EXERCISE 1: TRY DIVIDING THIS PARAGRAPH FROM HENRY DAVID THOREAU'S "THE BATTLE OF THE ANTS" INTO PHRASES. USE A SLASH (/) BETWEEN PHRASES TO SHOW WHERE THE DIVISIONS ARE. I WILL DO THE FIRST FEW TO GET YOU STARTED.

> "I took up the chip / on which the three I have described
> were struggling, / carried it /into my house, / and placed
> it under a tumbler on my window sill in order to see the
> issue. Holding a microscope to the first-mentioned red
> ant, I saw that, though he was assiduously gnawing at the
> near fore leg of his enemy, having severed his remaining
> feeler, his own breast was all torn away, exposing what
> vitals he had there to the jaws of the black warrior, whose
> breastplate was apparently too thick for him to pierce; and
> the dark carbuncles of the sufferer's eyes shown with
> ferocity such as war only could excite.

LYRIC PHRASES/MUSICAL PHRASES

Like a happily married couple, lyric phrases and musical phrases should match. Putting them out of sync with each other usually ends up in disaster.

The examples below are rewrites of actual songs. I have changed enough words to protect the innocent (or maybe the guilty). The brackets show how long the *musical phrases* are. Slashes show where the lyric phrases are.

[Some days it's simple/ but some days it's not/]

[Sometimes I wonder if there's *one thing we've got*]

[*In common*/ to stop us from drifting apart/]

"One thing we've got in common" sounds very strange when it is set in separate musical phrases. It is distracting and takes away from the emotion in the song. Like a love affair between opposites, it is an interesting but doomed experiment.

Here is another example:

[I know *your schemes*]

[Don't include me/].

There is a big difference between saying

1. "I know your schemes. Please don't include me.

and saying

2. "I know (that) your schemes don't include me."

Decide which one you mean, and then write your musical phrases to match. When musical phrases and lyric phrases are the same length, problems do not crop up.

BALANCING/UNBALANCING

If you count, you will find eight short phrases in the verse of "Your Gold Teeth II." If you count their combinations into longer phrases, you will find four. Either way, the even number of phrases helps make the structure feel balanced. An odd number of phrases would seem awkward:

Who are these children
who scheme and run wild
who speak with their wings
and the way that they smile
what are the secrets
they trace in the sky
each time they ride by

It would have seemed balanced if it had been:

Who are these children
who scheme and run wild
who speak with their wings
and the way that they smile

or even if it had been:

Who are these children
who scheme and run wild
who speak with their smiles
what are the secrets
they trace in the sky
each time they ride by.

If you look at the way phrases stack up into sections, you will have a better understanding of balance. Still, you may ask what difference it makes when a section is balanced or unbalanced.

The answer is that *unbalanced* sections create *a sense of forward movement,* while *balanced sections stop the motion.* Like a juggler, you rely on moving and stopping to create special effects in your act. Balancing or unbalancing sections of your lyric can serve at least three purposes:

1. Spotlight important ideas,
2. Moving one section forward into another section,
3. Contrasting one section with another one.

Look at each of these:

1. *Spotlighting important ideas*

This is the easiest and most practical use of balancing. When a section has an even number of phrases, the last phrase, the balancing position, is a perfect place for important ideas because it is a place where the lyric structure stops moving. It shines a spotlight on whatever you put there. You should use the position well. Here is a simple example from Buck Ram:

> Yes I'm the GREAT PRETENDER
>
> Pretending that I'm doing well
>
> My need is such, I pretend too much
>
> I'm lonely but no one can tell

The last phrase is in the even-numbered position, balancing the section. This position spotlights the last idea, "I'm lonely but no one can tell." It seems to be a very important idea, almost a summary of the section. So putting it in balancing position spotlights it effectively.

As a writer you must decide which ideas are most important, and then put them where they are the most likely to be noticed. The balancing position is always a good place.

EXERCISE 2: REARRANGE THE FOLLOWING EXAMPLES SO THE MOST IMPORTANT IDEA (TO YOU) IS IN THE BALANCING OR STOPPING POSITION. (RIGHT NOW "LOVELY AS A SONG" IS SPOTLIGHTED.)

    a. WOMEN OF THE EVENING (Keep this here)

       Help you get along

       Here and then they're gone

       Lovely as a song

Rewrite:

    b. If you think you need me

       If you want to please me

       Try another time

       Learn to read the signs

Rewrite:

2. *Moving one section forward into another section*

Moving is important when you intend to connect one unbalanced section to another equally unbalanced section. The example below balances three phrases with three more phrases:

> Who are these children
> who scheme and run wild
> who speak with their smiles
> what are the secrets
> they trace in the sky
> each time they ride by.

Using an odd number of phrases to unbalance a section works wonders if you want to build up pressure, for example, in a transitional section between verse and chorus.

> Baby can you see it
> Baby can you see it
> Baby can you see it

Repeating the *same* phrase three times creates dramatic movement, but you can get the same effect using different phrases too. The pressure to move forward builds up simply because you feel the need for a balancing position.

> One more time to reach you
> One more time to touch you
> One more time to tell you

EXERCISE 3: TAKE AWAY A PHRASE OR ADD A PHRASE TO UNBALANCE EACH OF THE EXAMPLES BELOW.

Example: Look at Mr. Smart Guy
    Cheating in school
    Stealing it from someone else
    Playing it cool

Rewrite: Look at Mr. Smart Guy
    Cheating in school
    Playing it cool

Your turn.

  a. Unlist your number
    Slip under cover
    Split for the summer
    Take on a lover

Rewrite:

      b.   I wonder who you're seeing in your dreams
           What fantasies you follow in your sleep
           I'll watch beside you till the morning light
           While you go chasing shadows through the night

Rewrite:

3.   *Contrasting one section with another one.*

This is the third practical use of balancing. When you already have a balanced section, you can write another section to match it except at the end, where you unbalance it, usually by adding another phrase.

THE GREAT PRETENDER

by Buck Ram

verse 1:   O yes I'm THE GREAT PRETENDER
             Pretending that I'm doing well
             My need is such, I pretend too much
             I'm lonely but no one can tell

verse 3:   Yes I'm THE GREAT PRETENDER
             Just laughing and gay like a clown
             I seem to be what I'm not, you see
             I'm wearing my heart like a crown
             Pretending that you're still around

In this case the extra phrase in the last verse is a surprise. Of course, the balancing position in verse three is spotlighted, but the surprise extra phrase spotlights both lines, especially the last phrase.

This unbalancing strategy is also useful when you have two verses that lead into a chorus. Make the first verse completely balanced, then unbalance the second verse by adding an extra phrase. This unbalancing will make it move forward into the chorus. The first and second verses of Kevin Cronin's "CAN'T FIGHT THIS FEELING" provide a good example.

      I can't fight this feeling any longer
      And yet I'm still afraid to let it flow
      What started out as friendship has grown stronger
      I only wish I had the strength to let it show

      I tell myself that I can't hold out forever
      I say there is no reason for my fear
      'Cause I feel so secure when we're together
      You give my life direction
      You make everything so clear →

Unbalancing the second verse makes it move forward. It throws it into the air, just like juggling. Notice that if you reverse the two verses, the motion stops.

EXERCISE 4:

A. UNBALANCE THE SECOND VERSE OF THE FOLLOWING EXAMPLE BY INSERTING EXTRA PHRASES TO MAKE IT MOVE FORWARD.

> verse 1:   Some girls have the restless touch
> Way they hold you lets you know
> They'll get you burning for a while
> Start you up and let you go

> verse 2:   Some girls have the leaving touch
> They'll hold you once and move along
> It's hard to keep 'em satisfied
> Morning comes and soon they're gone

Revision of verse 2:

B. BALANCE THE SECOND VERSE OF THE FOLLOWING EXAMPLE TO MAKE THE MOTION STOP.

> verse 1:   Gold from Acapulco
> '49 Desoto
> Running for the border
> Partners in crime
> Danger's getting closer
> Go a little slower
> Engine's overheating
> Starting to whine

> verse 2:   Agents from the Bureau
> Treacherous and thorough
> Waiting at the crossing
> Biding their time
> Moving to surround us
> Desperation hounds us
> Closing in around us
> Trouble coming down now
> Close to the line

Revision of verse 2:

CHAPTER TWO
LENGTH OF PHRASES: CONTROLLING YOUR SPEED

Now that you have your balance, it is time to work on speed. Like a juggler, your goal is not to get faster, but to control your speed. The length of your phrases is one of your most potent speed controllers.

Limericks are the most familiar systems that use phrase length to create speed.

> There once was a student named Esser
>
> Whose knowledge grew lesser and lesser
>
> It at last grew so small
>
> He knew nothing at all
>
> And now he's a college professor

The shorter third and fourth phrases of a limerick accelerate the movement. Speeding up right before the punchline adds to the humor when we get there.

Longer-than-usual phrases slow structures down. They throw the balance off.

> One by one
>
> Step by step
>
> We fall into the pit of despair
>
> One by one

The long third phrase slows the pace down, setting us up to pitch headlong into the pit at line four.

Speeding up and slowing down are relative ideas. Longer phrases must be longer than *something*. Shorter phrases must be shorter than *something*. You must establish a pace before you can speed up or slow down. The contrast is what gives you control.

Keeping all the phrases the same length keeps the pace *constant*.

EXERCISE 5: PUT AN "X" IN THE RIGHT BLANK TO DESCRIBE THE EFFECT OF THE PHRASE LENGTHS ON THE PACE OF EACH STRUCTURE.

1. Be still my beating heart

   It would be better to be cool

   It's not time to be open just yet

   A lesson once learned is so hard to forget

   — Sting, "BE STILL MY BEATING HEART"

   __ CONSTANT __ ACCELERATED _X_ DECELERATED

2. And I let time go by so slow

   And I made every moment last

   And I thought about years

   How they take so long

   And go so fast

   — Beth Nielsen Chapman, "YEARS"

   __ CONSTANT __ ACCELERATED __ DECELERATED

3. When I left I left walking wounded
    I made my escape from the rain
    Still a prisoner of hurt
    I had months worth of work
    Freeing my mind of the pain
    I had hours of sitting alone in the dark
    Listening to sad songs and coming apart
    Lord knows I made crying an art
    Weak is a SLOW HEALING HEART
                    — Jim Rushing, "SLOW HEALING HEART"

___ CONSTANT ___ ACCELERATED ___ DECELERATED

4. You sure were something at the school homecoming
    Smiling with your top down in the big parade
    And I felt so proud I broke right down and cried
                    — Wendy Levy, "HOMECOMING"

___ CONSTANT ___ ACCELERATED ___ DECELERATED

Number three is complicated because it speeds up at

> Still a prisoner of hurt
> I had months worth of work,

and goes back to its earlier pace at

> Freeing my mind of the pain

and then, relative to the original phrase length, slows down at the phrases,

> I had hours of sitting alone in the dark
> Listening to sad songs and coming apart.

So you have to fill in more than one blank. Jim Rushing is a good juggler, in perfect control of his speed at all times. It is no accident that his longest phrases show us how slowly the time passes. It is no accident that Beth Nielsen Chapman's shortest phrase about years is,

> And go so fast.

"Prosody" means that things fit well with one another. Here, for example, how well meaning fits with structure. Here we're talking about the way syllables fit with melody in a song. It can also be used in other ways. "Slow Healing Heart" and "Years" are both wonderful examples of perfect prosody of meaning and structure.

EXERCISE 6: BELOW I GIVE YOU STARTING PHRASES. COMPLETE EACH SECTION IN TWO DIFFERENT WAYS: FIRST SO THAT THE SECTION ACCELERATES; THEN SO THAT IT DECELERATES. OF COURSE, USE PHRASE LENGTHS TO MAKE IT HAPPEN.

example: *I left you in the summertime*
               We never even said good-bye

ACCELERATED VERSION:

> I left you in the summertime
> We never even said goodbye
> I want you back
> I miss your touch
> I'm tired of these winter skies

(If you dropped the last phrase, you could still call the section accelerated, but it would be unbalanced.)

DECELERATED VERSION:

> I left you in the summertime
> I never even said goodbye
> Now winter skies foretell the coming cold
> And I remain to shiver all alone

Your turn.

1. I've been playing cards all night
    I'll never get it right

ACCELERATED VERSION:

DECELERATED VERSION:

2. The last time that I saw you
    Your hair was up in curls
    Never saw you lookin' quite so nice

ACCELERATED VERSION:

DECELERATED VERSION:

3. Caught you lookin'
   Dead to rights
   Something's cookin'

ACCELERATED VERSION:

DECELERATED VERSION:

4. Lost your love by playing hard to get
   Tried to win and gave away the set

ACCELERATED VERSION:

DECELERATED VERSION:

Contrasting Sections

You can speed up from one section to another by making the phrases in the second section shorter:

Lovin' ain't no fashion show	VERSE
Changing all the time	
Put it on, take it off	
Struttin' down the line	
Love ain't just another fad	
In and out of style	
Outta feel like part of you	
Mile after mile	

SKIN TIGHT	CHORUS
Fits right	
Nice and snug	
SKIN TIGHT	
Pure delight	
Can't get close enough	
SKIN TIGHT	
All night	
Wrap me up in love	
SKIN TIGHT	

Or this:

If I went into analysis	VERSE
And took myself apart	
And laid me out for both of us to see	
You'd go into paralysis	
Right there in my arms	
Finding out you're not a bit like me	

READY OR NOT	CHORUS
We've got what we've got	
Let's give it a shot	
READY OR NOT	

You can feel the prosody. In the first example the short phrases are in the "snug" section. In the second example, the intellectualism in longer phrases contrasts with shorter, more active phrases in the chorus.

Randy Newman gets the opposite effect in "MY OLD KENTUCKY HOME."

VERSE

Turpentine and dandelion wine

I've turned the corner and I'm doing fine

Shooting at birds on the telephone line

Picking them off with this gun of mine

I got a fire in my belly and a fire in my head

Going higher and higher 'till I'm dead

CHORUS

> Oh the sun shines bright on MY OLD KENTUCKY HOME
>
> And the young folks roll on the floor
>
> Oh the sun shines bright on MY OLD KENTUCKY HOME
>
> Keep them hard times away from my door

The ideas in the verse are fast and funny, in shorter phrases. The chorus just leans back on the haystack in longer phrases. Again, nice prosody.

EXERCISE 7: I WILL GIVE YOU A WHOLE SECTION. CONTINUE FROM WHERE I LEAVE OFF AND WRITE ANOTHER SECTION WITH SHORTER PHRASES. MAKE YOUR IDEAS APPROPRIATE FOR THE ACCELERATED SECTION. THEN, GO BACK AND WRITE A SLOWER SECTION WITH LONGER PHRASES. AGAIN, TRY FOR PROSODY. YOU CAN EITHER WRITE BALANCED OR UNBALANCED STRUCTURES, WHICHEVER IS MORE APPROPRIATE.

example:
> Love me like a candy bar
>
> Sugar, try my flavors
>
> Let me be your chocolate star
>
> Layer after layer

ACCELERATED SECTION continuing from the original idea:

> My kisses are sticky
>
> Take them quickly
>
> I'll melt in your hands
>
> If you don't make some plans

DECELERATED SECTION continuing from the original idea:

> Oh Henry I'll be Forever Yours
>
> Till Mars deserts the Milky Way
>
> And kids desert the candy stores
>
> Oh Henry, I've lost my self-control
>
> Get ready for a marathon
>
> Make your tootsie roll

Your turn.

1. The sidewalk sure looks different
   When moonlight splashes down
   Sliding by in patterns as I move
   I like the feeling late at night
   With no one else around
   And all I hear's the clicking of my shoes

ACCELERATED SECTION continuing from the original idea:

DECELERATED SECTION continuing from the original idea:

2. I've been fogged out bogged down
    Tongue tripped spun around
    Waking shaking dust from my brain
    Dr. Feel Good's dead wood's
    Slinkin' 'round the neighborhood
    Promising relief from the pain

ACCELERATED SECTION continuing from the original idea:

DECELERATED SECTION continuing from the original idea:

3. We're always meeting secretly
    Keeping out of sight
    Knowing that we can't be seen
    Knowing what we do ain't right

ACCELERATED SECTION continuing from the original idea:

DECELERATED SECTION continuing from the original idea:

Exercises like these give you control over speed and balance. They help make PROSODY a practical possibility, rather than something you reach only by instinct or accident.

Watch Gary Nicholson and John Jarvis juggle two balls at once in the first two verses of "FATHERS AND SONS."

> My father had so much to tell me
>
> Things he said I ought to know
>
> Don't make my mistakes
>
> There are rules you can't break
>
> But I had to find out on my own
>
> Now when I look at my own son
>
> I know what my father went through
>
> There's only so much you can do
>
> You're proud when they walk
>
> Scared when they run
>
> That's how it always has been between FATHERS AND SONS

The first verse is more or less a limerick form, which is perfectly all right for serious lyrics. (When lyrics are set to music, the musical rhythms dominate and the limerick feeling is shaded.) It seems balanced in spite of the odd number of phrases, since, as you saw earlier, the two short phrases sort of add up to one long one.

The first verse has nice prosody. The phrases quoting the father's advice are short: typically, advice is barely heard by the son.

> Don't make my mistakes
>
> There are rules you can't break

In the second verse they add a phrase

> There's only so much you can do

to throw the structure off balance. After the extra phrase, the two short phrases that follow

> You're proud when they walk
>
> Scared when they run

feel lopsided, a little like a small child careening across a yard, barely able to keep his feet under him. Then the coup de grace:

> That's how it always has been between FATHERS AND SONS

This line decelerates dramatically because of its length, calling all kinds of attention to the part of the phrase that hangs over. It just happens to be the title of the song. We are still off balance from all of this, and are then moved into a very regular and secure chorus. Nice, huh? Great prosody. Great writing.

CHAPTER THREE
RHYTHM: SETTING UP, SHUTTING DOWN

> Sink like a stone that's been thrown in the ocean
>
> My logic has drowned in a sea of emotion
>
> Stop before you start
>
> BE STILL MY BEATING HEART
>
> —Sting, "Be Still My Beating Heart"

SYLLABLES

To understand lyric rhythm, we have to understand its basic building blocks, syllables. OK, this is pretty basic stuff, but we should make sure our footing is solid since we are headed for some slippery territory. From syllables we will go on to stressed and unstressed syllables, and only then to rhythm — stressed and unstressed syllables organized into patterns.

Syllables are the basic building blocks of all language. A syllable is usually made up of one vowel sound and one or more consonant sounds. Here are some syllables.

jo   give   set   strength   un   peace

A syllable does not have be a word, but all words have to be at least one syllable. The syllables above all have a vowel sound, some with a consonant before the vowel sound, some with a consonant after the vowel sound, and some with consonants both before and after the vowel sound. Sometimes a syllable has only a vowel sound with no consonants at all:

I   a   mel - *o* - dy

In one case, a syllable has two vowel sounds, slurred together and treated as a single vowel. We call it a diphthong.

boil   pail   out   now

Since diphthongs contain two vowel sounds, composers often use two notes to set them to music. Syllables containing only one vowel sound typically are set to one note.

EXERCISE 8: BREAK EACH OF THE FOLLOWING WORDS INTO SYLLABLES IN THE SPACE PROVIDED.

1. careless: *care less*
2. intimidate:
3. relief:
4. understatement:
5. melodramatic:
6. splurged:
7. stopped:
8. hone:
9. flower:
10. lease:

If you do not have a dictionary handy, stop here and go out and buy one. It is a tool of your trade. If you own one, go get it. Are you back? Good. Now, look up the words above. Most dictionaries divide syllables after the listing.

A basic rule for dividing words: while there are exceptions, syllables with short vowels usually attach the next consonant to the short vowel (man-u-script, not ma-nu-script), while syllables with long vowels divide between the long vowel and the consonant (ta-ble, not tab-le; re-lief, not rel-ief).

As you noticed in your dictionary, words with two or more syllables have a mark over one of the syllables. The mark indicates the word's main STRESS or emphasis. In English, all words of two or more syllables have a syllable that is stressed more than those around it. This gives words of two or more syllables a sonic "shape" to help your ear hear groups of syllables that "go together." Stressed syllables differ from the unstressed syllables in three ways: a stressed syllable is

a) higher in pitch
b) louder
c) longer

than the unstressed syllables around it. In effect, words of two or more syllables have a little melody, with the stressed syllable "on the beat." That's how we learn them.

Pronounce the word "incision" (in cí sion) as naturally as you can five times. Now, slow down and listen to yourself. You can hear differences between the syllables. "Ci" is higher, louder, and longer than the other two.

ciiii
in   sion

There is a simple reason for these little melodies. They give us an extra way to identify words during conversations, without the speaker having to pause between words. Our ear recognizes not only the sounds of the words, but also their shapes. When several syllables go together to make up a word, its shape helps us to recognize it as one word. This feature of multi-syllable words is called CONVENTIONAL STRESS because we all, as speakers of English, *agree* to organize our words in these particular ways. Our conventions are registered in our book of agreements, the dictionary.

EXERCISE 9: Divide the following words into syllables. Mark the stressed syllable by placing a diagonal slash (∕) above the vowel of the stressed syllable.

1. quiet: *quí et*
2. imbed:
3. refreshing:
4. number:
5. present (verb):
6. present (noun):
7. suspicious:
8. suspect (verb):
9. suspect (noun):
10. perfect (verb):

Again, check your work using your dictionary.

In three syllable words, when the strongest or PRIMARY STRESS is on the first syllable (as in "turbulent") or on the last syllable (as in "understand"), we give the syllable at the opposite end of the word a SECONDARY STRESS (∕∕). The Secondary Stress is stronger than the middle syllable, so it gives the word shape. In

túr bŭ lént

the third syllable gets the Secondary Stress. In

ún dĕr stánd

the first syllable gets the Secondary Stress. The idea is that, in English, we tend to speak in patterns of alternating stressed and unstressed syllables.

When the primary stress is on the middle syllable, there is no secondary stress.

re lín quĭsh

jŭ dí cious

Words of four or more syllables will always have Secondary Stress.

EXERCISE 10: DIVIDE THESE WORDS INTO SYLLABLES AND MARK BOTH THE PRIMARY STRESS AND THE SECONDARY STRESS IN EACH WORD. PLACE "∕" OVER THE SYLLABLE WITH PRIMARY STRESS AND "∕∕" OVER THE SYLLABLE WITH SECONDARY STRESS.

1. un re lént ing:
2. everpresent:
3. intimidating:
4. fortunately:
5. competent:
6. understandably:
7. consummate:
8. delicatessen:
9. intimately:
10. misunderstanding:

So far we haven't considered ordinary one-syllable words. They are the staple of English (and more so for lyrics, since most lyrics try for direct and simple language). How do we know whether a one-syllable word is stressed or not? Though we can look in a dictionary for the stressed syllable of a multi-syllable word, the dictionary says nothing about one-syllable words.

Stress for one-syllable words depends on what their job is in a phrase. Very roughly, words do two kinds of jobs. If they carry meaning ("semantic" function — nouns, verbs, adjectives, adverbs), they are stressed. For example, these words will always be stressed:

track   list   risk   luck   slick   hard   stem   strip

This is called STRESS BY IMPORTANCE.

When words work simply as grammatical road signs to show relationships *between* words (grammatical function), they are unstressed. The grammatical function is very important. The opening lines of Lewis Carroll's "Jabberwocky"

'Twas brillig, and the slithy toves

Did gyre and gimble in the wabe;

—from "Alice Through the Looking Glass."

seem to make sense. Of course they don't, because the sounds "brillig," "slithy," "toves," "gimble," and "wabe" are not connected to any ideas. So why do the lines seem to say something? The answer is in the unstressed syllables. They tweak our ears; tell us to get ready for certain kinds of words.

'Twas _____(predicate adjective)_____ and the _____(noun cluster)_____

Did __(verb)__ and __(verb)__ in the _____(place where, noun or adj.)_____ ;

We know from the unstressed words what to expect next. And even though we cannot understand the meaning of "gimble," we know it is something you do, which gives it the shadow of meaning it seems to have.

These unstressed words make it easier to carry on efficient conversations. A millisecond before we hear a word, we already know what kind of a word it will be. This cuts down the odds of making a mistake.

The list of Grammatical Functions includes *prepositions (e.g.,* of, to, after, over), *articles (e.g.,* a, an, the), *conjunctions* (e.g., and, or, but), *auxiliary verbs indicating tense (e.g.,* have run, *had* run), *auxiliary verbs indicating mood* (e.g. *might* run, *may* run), *personal pronouns* (e.g., I, him, their), and *relative pronouns* (e.g., which, who, when). Most of the time, these words are unstressed.

There are exceptions. Grammatical Functions can be stressed when some sort of *contrast* between them is stated or implied:

I asked you to throw the ball tó me, not át me.

I asked you to throw the ball to mé, not to hér.

I asked yóu to throw the ball, not hím.

These are the only times unstressed one-syllable words are stressed to show their importance. Exceptions are usually pretty clear when they happen. Most of the time, one-syllable words are stressed only when they communicate ideas; when they are "meaning carriers."

EXERCISE 11: MARK THE STRESSED WORDS WITH "╱" OVER THE VOWEL OF THE STRESSED SYLLABLE. MARK UNSTRESSED SYLLABLES WITH "◡" OVER THE VOWEL. IF THERE ARE SECONDARY STRESSES IN MULTI-SYLLABLE WORDS, PUT THEM IN.

1. For the first few, let's stick with prose.
2. Mark the stressed syllables with a slash.
3. Use a slight cup to show unstressed words or parts of words.
4. In the still of the night I got light-headed.
5. This stuff is a snap.
6. Words like "of" and "and" can throw you.
7. When I got home the house was dark.
8. Don't tell me you want me if you don't want to keep me.
9. I saw you once and that was it; I felt my knees go weak.
10. Listen to what I say, not to the guy next to you.

The answers are not always clear, especially when you have strings of one-syllable words. Shades of interpretation and intention can make a difference. Don't *panic.* There are often grey areas where it is hard to judge a word's importance, but it is usually easy to pick out the most *important words* and intentions anyway.

When I got home the house was dark.

Some parts are totally clear. Start with those.

When I got hóme the house wăs dárk.

"When" probably isn't stressed. "I" could be stressed if someone else was coming home. "Got" could be stressed if the lights came on (maybe a surprise party) soon afterwards. But most likely, we are looking at

Whĕn Ĭ gŏt hóme thĕ house wăs dárk.

Although it may not be perfectly clear what the first three syllables *are,* it is very clear what they *are not.* They *are not* the most important syllables in the phrase — typical for words in grey areas. There would be no problem setting this phrase to music — just save the important places in the measures for the most important words. You know what they are. The rest will work out with a little trial and error.

Remember that looking for stressed syllables is a matter of seeing the stresses that are there rather than *forcing* a pattern onto the phrase. In poetry, the process of identifying stress patterns is called "scansion" or "scanning." We will use the same term.

EXERCISE 12: SCAN THE FOLLOWING EXAMPLES FOR STRESSED AND UNSTRESSED SYLLABLES. MARK STRESSED SYLLABLES WITH "′", SECONDARY STRESSES (WHERE APPROPRIATE IN MULTI-SYLLABLE WORDS) WITH "″", AND UNSTRESSED SYLLABLES WITH "◡".

1. Time to say goodbye to the old crowd. Split with the boys up the alley to the yard.
2. Suddenly you're lost and you just can't help it.
3. Goodbye sweet child, it'll get you too.
4. Going out dancing, looking like a party girl.
5. Our time was spent too quickly, winnowed by the wind.

PATTERNS

Now we can look at the third ball. Once you start putting syllables into patterns, you are mixing the rhythmic element with phrase length and number of phrases.

Lyrics are "married" to music. Whether the lyric is written *before* the music, at the *same time* as the music, or *after* the music, its syllables are intended to fit with notes. Music is, by its nature, rhythmic. So you must arrange syllables into rhythmic patterns, either to *prepare* them for music or to *match* music that has already been written.

You will spend a lot of writing time trying to match patterns — patterns of notes, or patterns you have written in earlier phrases or sections of your lyric: for example, matching your second verse with your first verse.

Suppose you had written the verse that opened this chapter (by Sting) and now want to match it. First, you would scan its phrases.

> Sink like a stone that's been thrown in the ocean
> My logic has drowned in a sea of emotion
> Stop before you start
> Be still my beating heart

These are pretty regular. The first two phrases are written in three-syllable patterns, the last two in two-syllable patterns. (Do you detect any prosody?)

It is important not to be greedy: do not put stressed syllables in the *unstressed* positions. This one is too hot.

> Cast *deep* in silence I can't *hold* my balance
> My weak *heart* revealed by the heat *born* of malice
> Devil *haunts* my past
> God give me peace at last

The "greedy" spots would surely get buried or at the very least sound hurried (and lose their emotion) when you set them to the music of the original verse.

It is equally important to match the original's important words with equally important words. This one is too cold:

> Yet in your silence I've *just* got my balance
> My weakness is *now* in the *place* of your malice
> Won't you help me past
> And *get* me *out* at last

This should be enough to lose anyone's interest.

You must resist greed. But you must put your important words in the important positions. This one is just right.

> Cast in your silence I'm losing my balance
> My weakness revealed by the heat of your malice

Devil in my past
Oh give me peace at last

This version should work with the music for the original words. The stresses match, and the most important words are in the same places.

EXERCISE 13: SCAN THE FOLLOWING PHRASES FOR STRESSED AND UNSTRESSED SYLLABLES. MARK THEM AS USUAL. THEN, WRITE *YOUR OWN PHRASES* TO MATCH THE STRESS PATTERNS OF THE ORIGINALS. WHERE YOU RUN INTO GREY AREAS, CREATE GREY AREAS OF YOUR OWN TO MATCH THEM. PUT YOUR MOST IMPORTANT WORDS IN THE SAME POSITION AS THE MOST IMPORTANT WORDS IN THE EXAMPLE.

1. You had your special perfume on when I got home.
Pattern match:

2. I'd rather be back in second place than no place in your heart.
Pattern match:

3. He knew he must defend the land: fight son to son, hand to hand.
Pattern match:

4. What made you think that we'd fall in love forever?
Pattern match:

5. One by one we reach for the chances, helpless as we sail away, out of time.
Pattern match:

6. He never was a bad boy, for he never was a child.
Pattern match:

7. If we're wrong, please don't show it. Keep me blind.
Pattern match:

8. Don't go down by yourself — Take somebody else to ease your mind.
Pattern match:

9. If only you believe it will be, it will be. Believe.
Pattern match:

10. I will never believe you. You're just playing a part. I know you've been leaving me in your heart.
Pattern match:

RHYTHM

To create a rhythm, simply repeat a pattern. Sometimes the pattern is small:

/ ◡   (DUM da)

If you repeat it a few times,

/ ◡ / ◡ / ◡

(DUM da DUM da DUM da DUM da)

Presto! A rhythmic figure.
The patterns can be larger:

/ ◡ ◡ /

repeated, you get

/ ◡ ◡ / / ◡ ◡ / / ◡ ◡ / / ◡ ◡ /

another rhythmic figure. The size of the pattern is not important. What is important is that the *pattern is repeated enough to make you expect it again.* The more even and regular the pattern is, the more quickly expectations lock in.

Let's start with alternating weak and strong syllables.

◡ / ◡ /

This is a very simple pattern based on the repetition of two elements. It is called a duple pattern.

◡ /

The simpler the repeated pattern, the quicker you get used to it. You get used to simple duples fast. Even after four beats, you begin to expect duples, and your PACE is set. Your PACE will be CONSTANT as long as you stay in duples.

◡ / ◡ / ◡ / ◡ /
◡ / ◡ / ◡ / ◡ /

If you change to triples the PACE speeds up (ACCELERATION). In the third and fourth phrases below:

I've been through every single book I know
Soothe the thoughts that plague me so
Sink like a stone that's been thrown in the ocean
My logic has drowned in a sea of emotion

On the other hand, if you change to *fewer* unstressed syllables, the PACE slows down (DE-CELERATION).

◡ / ◡ / ◡ / ◡ /
◡ / ◡ / ◡ / ◡ /
/ / / /

This is easy to understand. If you set the above structures to music, you would normally set the strong stresses in musically strong rhythmic positions. The strong stresses stay in the same places even when unstressed syllables are added or taken away. Adding unstressed syllables "crowds" in between the strong stresses, demanding short notes that move faster. When you take away unstressed syllables, the spaces between the stresses "open up," slowing down to allow longer notes or rests between notes.

If you start with triples and change to duples, the PACE slows down

> Sínk like a stóne that's been thrówn in the ócean
> My lógic has drówned in a séa of emótion
> Stóp befóre you stárt
> Be still my béating héart

The *rhythm* slows in the third and fourth phrases. The acceleration you might hear is caused by *phrase length,* the second ball we juggled.

(Now we can be more precise when we say one phrase is "longer" or "shorter" than another one. When you want to know how long a phrase is, you can figure it out accurately, not by counting *syllables,* but by counting *stressed syllables.* For example, ∪ / ∪ / ∪ / ∪ / is *longer* than ∪ ∪ / ∪ ∪ / ∪ ∪ /, even though it has one less syllable. If you set the two to music, ∪ / ∪ / ∪ / ∪ / will extend further.)

Once you start repeating phrases, structures start to form, creating dynamics and motion. The balls juggle easily. Watch.

> / ∪ / ∪ / ∪
> / ∪ / ∪ /
> / ∪ / ∪ / ∪

Constant duples keep you moving. The phrases stack up in an unbalanced threesome, with the second one shorter. When you hear the third phrase matching the first phrase exactly, you expect that the "odd" phrase

> / ∪ / ∪ /

will follow, just as it followed the first longer phrase.

What if the "odd" phrase does not appear again? You would feel unsatisfied. Depending on what *did* appear, the structure would at least be unbalanced, it might even be unresolved or *open.* As you can now see, there is a little more to the idea of BALANCE than simply the number of phrases.

If the "odd" phrase appears, you will be satisfied. The structure will be resolved or CLOSED.

When we put these four phrases together, the result is a very common structure we will use as a standard, or "PARADIGM." You will use it and its variations as long as you write lyrics.

PARADIGM 1:   / ∪ / ∪ / ∪ /
/ ∪ / ∪ /   → motion
/ ∪ / ∪ / ∪ /   → motion
/ ∪ / ∪ /   ← closure

This structure, alternating four-stress and three-stress phrases, has a name: Common Meter. It is the most familiar rhythm pattern in English. This example fits our paradigm almost perfectly:

> Máry hád a líttle lámb
> Its fléece was whíte as snów
> And éverywhére that Máry wént
> The lámb was súre to gó

The secondary stress on "everywhere" does not change the pattern. Treat secondary stresses just like a strong stress. The unaccented syllable opening lines two, three, and four work as pickups; they do not change the pattern either.

If you try to stop anywhere along the way in Common Meter, you will feel unsatisfied. It keeps you going until it ends.

> Máry hád a líttle lámb
> Its fléece was whíte as snów

As you can see, this is unbalanced. You cannot stop here. If it were

> Mary had a little lamb
> Its fleece was white as whitest snow

it would be rhythmically balanced. You could stop.

> Mary had a little lamb
> Its fleece was white as snow
> And everywhere that Mary went

It is impossible to stop here. You must continue forward. But not only do you need to go ahead, *you already know where you should end up!* You expect, and GET

> The lamb was sure to go

If it had ended any other way you would have been surprised.

Common Meter is still alive and well today on every Billboard chart. It is the most common meter, especially for lyrics, since it works so perfectly outlining the different subdivisions of the 8-bar phrase. If you set the stressed syllables of each phrase of Common Meter in the stressed quarter-note positions of bars of 4/4 time, the first phrase becomes

fitting perfectly into the 2-bar phrase. Line 2 becomes

The silent third beat of the fourth bar serves to define phrase two's difference from phrase one, and at the same time uses the silence to define the four-bar phrase. Phrase three repeats phrase one:

defining the third two-bar phrase, and raising your expectations for the final two bars:

which brings the system to a smooth and firm conclusion. It adds up to an eight-bar phrase, and it also defines along the way subdivisions of two-bar and four-bar phrases.

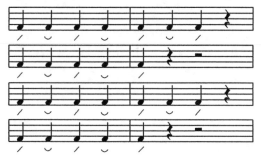

What meter could be better than Common Meter for popular music, since popular music is normally written in divisions and subdivisions of two, four, and eight bars?

Common Meter will be a PARADIGM, a *standard form you will use as a reference point,* when you put structures together. The advantage of using paradigms is that they create very clear effects. They help you see how other structures work.

PARADIGM 1: ╱ ◡ ╱ ◡ ╱ ◡ ╱   (or, in triples)   ╱ ◡ ◡ ╱ ◡ ◡ ╱ ◡ ◡ ╱

╱ ◡ ╱ ◡ ╱   ╱ ◡ ◡ ╱ ◡ ◡ ╱

╱ ◡ ╱ ◡ ╱ ◡ ╱   ╱ ◡ ◡ ╱ ◡ ◡ ╱ ◡ ◡ ╱

╱ ◡ ╱ ◡ ╱   ╱ ◡ ◡ ╱ ◡ ◡ ╱

We can describe the effects of Common Meter in terms of five concepts: BALANCE, PACE, FLOW, CLOSURE, and TYPE OF CLOSURE.

1. *BALANCE:* It is BALANCED — there is an even number of phrases, each phrase has a counterpart, and the order of the phrases is repeated. Nothing is left "hanging."

2. *PACE:* It moves in a CONSTANT duple pattern of stress/unstress, neither ACCELER-ATED nor DECELERATED.

3. *FLOW:* The structure is THROUGH-WRITTEN: that is, there is *no place of resolution* before the end of the last phrase. The structure keeps pushing you forward.

4. *CLOSURE:* It is CLOSED, or resolved. Your expectations are satisfied by the way the fourth phrase ends. You feel no need to continue on to another phrase. If there were a need to continue on, the structure would be OPEN.

5. *TYPE OF CLOSURE:* The resolution is EXPECTED. It is how you would have predicted (when you reached the end of phrase three) that the entire structure would end.

We have just developed what we will call the *STRUCTURAL PENTAD* (penta = "five") — five normal characteristics of any structure, be it a rhythmic structure, a rhyme structure, or even a musical structure. The full Structural Pentad, set up for easy handling, looks like this:

BALANCE: ___ SYMMETRICAL   ___ ASYMMETRICAL

PACE: ___ CONSTANT   ___ ACCELERATED   ___ DECELERATED

FLOW: ___ THROUGH-WRITTEN   ___ FRAGMENTED

CLOSURE: ___ CLOSED   ___ OPEN

C. TYPE: ___ EXPECTED   ___ UNEXPECTED   ___ DECEPTIVE

We can show the characteristics of Common Meter by simply placing "x" in the appropriate blanks.

BALANCE: _x_ SYMMETRICAL   ___ ASYMMETRICAL

PACE: _x_ CONSTANT   ___ ACCELERATED   ___ DECELERATED

FLOW: _x_ THROUGH-WRITTEN   ___ FRAGMENTED

CLOSURE: _x_ CLOSED   ___ OPEN

C. TYPE: _x_ EXPECTED   ___ UNEXPECTED   ___ DECEPTIVE

EXERCISE 14: USING PARADIGM ONE, WRITE THREE SYSTEMS, EACH WITH DIFFERENT CONTENT. SINCE PARADIGM ONE IS THROUGH-WRITTEN, TRY TO MAKE EACH SYSTEM CARRY ITS IDEA THROUGH TO THE END. WRITE ONE OF YOUR SYSTEMS IN TRIPLES.

1.

2.

3.

Here is another structure, stated in duples.

PARADIGM 2: / ⌣ / ⌣ / ⌣ /

                 / ⌣ / ⌣ / ⌣ / ← closure

                 / ⌣ / ⌣ / ⌣ /

                 / ⌣ / ⌣ / ⌣ / ← closure

As in:

> Eenie Meenie Minie Moe
>
> Catch a tiger by the toe
>
> If he hollers let him go
>
> Eenie Meenie Minie Moe

This is a close relative of Common Meter, but its effects are quite different. Most important, its second phrase has four stresses rather than three. PARADIGM TWO works by simple repetition rather than by repetition and variation like common meter. Common meter (PARADIGM ONE) works like this:

> SAME
>
> DIFFERENT
>
> SAME . . .

your expectation that phrase two will be repeated at the end is what keeps the system moving. On the other hand, PARADIGM TWO works like this:

> SAME
>
> SAME
>
> SAME
>
> SAME

Because there is no difference between phrase one and phrase two, there is no tension to keep the system moving. Because the number of phrases is BALANCED, the system closes *internally* after phrase two. When you set PARADIGM TWO in 4/4 bars, it defines a four-*bar unit as the primary unit* of the structure rather than, like Common Meter, showing the four-bar unit as a subdivision of an eight-bar unit. We can describe PARADIGM TWO as follows:

1. *BALANCE:* It is BALANCED — there is an even number of phrases, each phrase has a counterpart, and the order of the phrases is repeated. Nothing is left "hanging."

2. *PACE:* It moves in a CONSTANT pattern of stress/unstress, neither ACCELERATED nor DECELERATED.

3. *FLOW:* The structure is FRAGMENTED, that is, there is an *internal point of resolution.* The structure stops after the second phrase, and then starts over again.

4. *CLOSURE:* It is CLOSED, or resolved. (Twice, in fact). You are satisfied both at the end of the second phrase and at the end of the fourth phrase that there is no need to continue on.

5. *TYPE OF CLOSURE:* The resolution is EXPECTED. It is how you would have predicted (when you reached the end of phrase three) that the entire structure would end.

We can show the characteristics of PARADIGM TWO by simply placing "x" in the appropriate blanks.

BALANCE: <u>x</u> SYMMETRICAL   ___ ASYMMETRICAL

PACE: <u>x</u> CONSTANT   ___ ACCELERATED   ___ DECELERATED

FLOW: ___ THROUGH-WRITTEN   <u>x</u> FRAGMENTED

CLOSURE: <u>x</u> CLOSED   ___ OPEN

C. TYPE: <u>x</u> EXPECTED   ___ UNEXPECTED   ___ DECEPTIVE

EXERCISE 15: USING PARADIGM TWO, WRITE THREE SYSTEMS, EACH WITH DIFFERENT CONTENT. SINCE PARADIGM TWO IS FRAGMENTED, TRY TO DIVIDE IT INTO TWO IDEAS, EACH IN ITS OWN TWO-PHRASE SEGMENT. WRITE ONE OF YOUR SYSTEMS IN TRIPLES.

1.

2.

3.

Comparing PARADIGM 1 and PARADIGM 2 is the best way to understand FLOW. It shows when and why a structure pushes forward, and when and why it doesn't.

PARADIGM 1: / ᵕ / ᵕ / ᵕ /

                  / ᵕ / ᵕ /   →   motion

                  / ᵕ / ᵕ / ᵕ / →   motion

                  / ᵕ / ᵕ /   ←   closure

PARADIGM 2:   / ‿ / ‿ / ‿ /

                   / ‿ / ‿ / ‿ /   ←   closure

                   / ‿ / ‿ / ‿ /

                   / ‿ / ‿ / ‿ /   ←   closure

We can combine these two PARADIGMS and get different results:

DECEPTIVE CLOSURE

PARADIGM 3:   / ‿ / ‿ / ‿ /

                   / ‿ / ‿ /   →

                   / ‿ / ‿ / ‿ /   →

                   / ‿ / ‿ / ‿ /   ←

As in:

       Mary had a little lamb
       Its fleece was white as snow
       And everywhere that Mary went
       She sold the fleece to pay *the rent*

The second phrase of PARADIGM THREE, like Common Meter, is different from the first, so the structure has *no internal closure* at that point. It moves you *forward*, making the structure THROUGH-WRITTEN rather than FRAGMENTED. When you get to line four, you expect to see

           / ‿ / ‿ /.

Instead, you see

           / ‿ / ‿ / ‿ /.

The extra strong stress goes against your expectations. *You knew what you wanted,* and were fooled. The structure is still CLOSED because it repeats a familiar phrase length (you have seen twice in the section), but the resolution is DECEPTIVE.

       BALANCE: __ SYMMETRICAL   _x_ ASYMMETRICAL
       PACE: _x_ CONSTANT   __ ACCELERATED   __ DECELERATED
       FLOW: _x_ THROUGH-WRITTEN   __ FRAGMENTED
       CLOSURE: _x_ CLOSED   __ OPEN
       C. TYPE: __ EXPECTED   __ UNEXPECTED   _x_ DECEPTIVE

A DECEPTIVE resolution sets you up to expect a particular ending, but it doesn't come. Instead, the structure ends with *something else you have already seen in the system* (otherwise the system would not close at all). So, there are two conditions for a CLOSURE to be DECEPTIVE,

1. The system must raise expectations that it will be resolved in a certain way, and

2. The phrase that is actually used to resolve the system must already be in the structure.

Like this:

       We're always meeting secretly
       Keeping out of sight
       Knowing no one else can see
       Knowing something isn't right

The system implies a 3-stress resolution, making the rhythmic deception possible. Deception creates a position of high profile. It turns on whole banks of spotlights. Make sure you put something there that is worth looking at. PARADIGM THREE is a clear example of DECEPTIVE CLOSURE. The price of the deception is to unbalance the structure.

EXERCISE 16: USING PARADIGM THREE, WRITE THREE SYSTEMS. THIS TIME, PUT THEM TOGETHER TO TELL A STORY. (START WITH "WE'RE ALWAYS MEETING SECRETLY. . ." IF YOU WANT TO.) EACH SYSTEM SHOULD ADVANCE THE IDEA FURTHER, LIKE THE PARAGRAPHS OF AN ESSAY. SINCE PARADIGM THREE IS THROUGH-WRITTEN, MAKE THE CONTENT OF EACH SYSTEM CONTINUE TO THE END. ADDITIONALLY, SINCE THE DECEPTIVE FOURTH PHRASE CALLS SPECIAL ATTENTION TO ITSELF, TRY TO PUT THE MOST IMPORTANT IDEA OF EACH SYSTEM IN THAT POSITION.

1.

2.

3.

Once more we are making an important assumption in the way we have approached DECEPTION: *that the stressed syllables in a phrase all have the same note length in the musical bar, so* that extra stressed syllables extend the number of bars. If, on the other hand, the stressed syllables of

     Knowing something isn't right

were squeezed into the same number of bars as phrase two,

     Keeping out of sight

the result would be the opposite. The longer phrases would sound like ACCELERATION rather than DECELERATION. Let's move on.

UNEXPECTED CLOSURE

To classify a resolution as UNEXPECTED (as opposed to DECEPTIVE), there must be *no expectation for a specific resolution*. The idea is a simple one: if you don't expect anything, you can't be fooled. (You can, however, still be startled or surprised.)

  The most common UNEXPECTED CLOSURE for a rhythmic system is a system that closes, then repeats a phrase (usually the last):

     Yes I'm the Great Pretender

     Laughing and gay like a clown

     I seem to be what I'm not you see

     I'm wearing my heart like a crown ←

     Pretending that you're still around ←

Or this:

> She'll put you on the ropes
> She likes to get her kicks
> She'll take you by the throat
> Strangle all your hopes   ←
> She'll put you on the ropes   ←

When a system creates a place that surprises you — that gets a lot of attention, use it well. It is a good place to put important ideas.

EXERCISE 17: WRITE TWO SYSTEMS ENDING WITH UNEXPECTED CLOSURE.

1.

2.

By now you should have control of RHYTHM, the third ball. You have an important tool for controlling how structure starts, moves, and stops. Now let's add that last ball that we need to juggle. This is another big one.

CHAPTER FOUR
RHYME: TAKING TOTAL CONTROL

Rhyme is a powerhouse. It affects all parts of structure: BALANCE, PACE, FLOW, CLOSURE, AND CLOSURE TYPE. Lyrics, unlike poetry and prose, are made for the ear alone. Since rhyme is an aural (ear) effect, it is a perfectly suited tool for lyricists.

Rhyme is a connection between syllables, not words. When we say that syllables rhyme, we are saying three things:

1. The syllables' *vowel sounds* are the same,
2. Their *ending consonants* (if any) are the same, and,
3. Their *beginnings* are different.

The first condition says that the sound of the vowel is more important than the alphabet letter you see on the page. You cannot always tell by looking what *sound* a letter will have. For example, the "o" in "not" sounds different than the "o" in "only," while the "o" in "love" sounds the same as the "u" in "club." You have to listen rather than look.

The second condition specifies "(if any)" because not all syllables have final consonants (for example, "free" and "go"). But when rhyming syllables do have ending consonant sounds, the sounds have to be the same.

Finally, the third condition says that the syllables have to start in different ways. This is because rhyme works on the basic musical principle of tension/resolution — difference moving into sameness.

The beginnings of the syllables have to be different for you to notice their similar sounds. The reason is simple. When you hear a cheerleader yell

> "go! go! go! go! go!"

you pay attention only to the repetitions, not to the sounds of the syllables. No one in the entire stadium thinks "Hey! Those syllables *sound* the same!"

"IDENTITY" means that syllables start the same way. "Fuse/confuse" is not a rhyme, it is an IDENTITY. Your ear does not pay attention to the *sounds* of the syllables. There is no tension, no "difference" to be resolved by sameness. "Peace/piece" and "lease/police" are also Identities. The same sounds are repeated, just like a cheerleader's yell.

IDENTITY is so important that at least one popular rhyming dictionary lists identities together and tells you not to pick two words from the same list. For example, it lists "birthplace, commonplace, misplace, place, replace . . . " together. Your ear will not pay attention to their sounds. But if you said "ace, brace, chase, erase, face, disgrace, resting place," your ear pays close attention to the sounds. You are hearing rhymes: difference moving into sameness. Look at the conditions for rhyme again.

1. The syllables' *vowel sounds* are the same,
2. Their *ending consonants* (if any) are the same, and,
3. Their *beginnings* are different.

When these three conditions are met, call it PERFECT RHYME. As we explore rhyme further, we will look at other kinds of rhyme besides PERFECT RHYME. For now, though, that is all we will use.

EXERCISE 18: THINK UP THREE PERFECT RHYMES FOR EACH OF THE FOLLOWING SYLLABLES. YOUR RHYMES DO NOT HAVE TO BE WORDS.

1. lant   _____   _____   _____

2. ints   _____   _____   _____

3. rutch   _____   _____   _____

4. mose   _____   _____   _____

5. kate   _____   _____   _____

Rhymes are divided into two categories:

1. Masculine Rhymes: Rhymes between monosyllables; or between the stressed last syllables of multi-syllable words. (including secondary stress at the ends of multi-syllable words.)

    hit/bit, go/under*tow*, re*treat* /over*heat*

2. Feminine Rhymes: two-syllable rhymes, in which the second-last syllables are stressed and the final syllables are unstressed. The stressed syllables have to rhyme. The unstressed syllables may be either rhymes or identities:

    only/lonely, idéa/María, liver/give her

EXERCISE 19: PUT AN "M" AFTER THE MASCULINE RHYMES AND AN "F" AFTER THE FEMININE RHYMES.

1. enjoy/destroy

2. oblique/unique

3. artichoke/baroque

4. penetration/salvation

5. triple/cripple

6. hexagon/Rubicon

7. libretto/falsetto

8. deny/pacify

9. Jezebel/repel

10. appreciate/relate

RHYME SCHEME

The way rhymes are arranged in a lyric is called the lyric's RHYME SCHEME. Letters of the alphabet are used to notate the arrangement. For example,

> black/wall/attack/fall

is notated as "a b a b," "a" for the "ack" sound and "b" for the "all" sound.

> black/attack/wall/fall

is "a a b b."

> black/wall/release/fall

is "x a x a." "x" is always used to show unrhymed lines.

EXERCISE 20: NOTATE THE RHYME SCHEME OF EACH OF THE FOLLOWING LISTS. USE LETTERS (INCLUDING "X" FOR UNRHYMED WORDS) AFTER EACH WORD. USE "I" TO NOTATE IDENTITIES.

1. notation   a
    motivation   a
    increase   b
    police   b
    relation   a

2. heart
    report
    sing
    start
    retort
    fling
    ring

3. strong
    hear
    along
    throng
    wrong

4. unleash
    force
    McLeash
    horse
    Norse

5. understand
    allowed
    reprimand
    slow
    grow
    crowd

6. start
    return
    ease
    burn

7. lass
    follow
    sorrow
    borrow
    glass
    hollow

8. fool
    rule
    sunny
    rate
    state
    honey

Now that our basic definitions are out of the way, we can start to juggle.

RHYME STRUCTURE

Rhyme, used at the ends of phrases, is your most effective tool for controlling moving and stopping. I will show you rhyme's power over structure. After you understand its power, the question "Do I *have to* rhyme?" will sound pretty silly. The *real* question is, "How can I learn to use rhyme better?" Rhyme controls or helps to control each structural area:

I. Rhyme helps create BALANCE (symmetry), or lack of BALANCE (asymmetry) in a structure.

II. Rhyme controls the PACE of structures. (Acceleration, Deceleration, Constant Motion)

III. Rhyme controls the FLOW of phrases by stopping motion, or by keeping motion going.

IV. Rhyme controls the CLOSURE (or resolution).

V. Rhyme helps control TYPE OF CLOSURE. (EXPECTED CLOSURE, DECEPTIVE CLOSURE, UNEXPECTED CLOSURE.)

The better you understand the effects of rhyme, the more control you will have over your lyric's structure. We will look carefully at each of rhyme's effects on structure.

I. BALANCE

Rhyme makes a lyric move. It moves forward by raising expectations. It stops by satisfying them. For example,

> trim
>
> alive
>
> swim . . .

makes you want to hear another "ive" sound. You want to move forward.

> trim
>
> alive
>
> swim
>
> *dive*

The reason that "swim" pushes forward is because it repeats a sound you have already heard at the beginning of the series. You want to hear the rest of it. Watch.

> im
>
> ive
>
> im. . .

"Ive" came after "im" the first time, so you expect it to come again. Two effects work together to move the structure forward:

1. a desire for the repetition of a *sound,*

2. a desire for the repetition of an *order.*

This second desire feeds off our desire for symmetry or balance. That is why

> trim   a
>
> alive   b
>
> dive   b

is not balanced by:

> trim   a
>
> live   b
>
> dive   b
>
> swim   a

it is balanced by:

trim	a
alive	b
dive	b
swim	a
deprive	b
strive	b

or even,

trim	a
alive	b
dive	b
swim	a
strain	c
gain	c

As you can see, sometimes repeating a *series* is even more important than repeating a sound. That is how important your sense of balance is. These are balanced.

a	x	a	a	a	x
b	a	a	a	b	x
a	x		b	c	a
b	a		b	a	x
				b	x
				c	a

I suppose I could call them paradigms of BALANCE. They all deliver the same thing:

1. the repetition of *sounds*.
2. the repetition of *order*.

EXERCISE 21: BALANCE THE FOLLOWING LISTS BY ADDING OR SUBTRACTING WORDS. TRY TO FIND RHYMES THAT MAKE SENSE WITH THE WORDS ALREADY THERE.

1. niece	2. decide	3. fulfill
stumble	ride	returning
fleece	course	unlock
crumble		will
peace		burning

4. revive	5. showing	6. confirm
connive	date	squirm
trick	gate	term
alive	mate	last
	glowing	

II. PACE

Rhyme is like the accelerator in a car: the closer the accelerator gets to the floor, the faster the car moves. The closer rhymes are to each other, the faster your lyric moves. And, like the accelerator and the car floor, the further apart they are, the slower you move.

Remember that speeding up and slowing down are relative terms. There has to be a reference point. For example,

> bring
>
> search
>
> sing

sets a PACE of *alternating* rhyme (every other line). It is waiting for an "urch" word. If you put in *consecutive* rhymes like

> bring
>
> search
>
> sing
>
> last
>
> *fast*

you ACCELERATE the system. If you set the PACE with consecutive rhyme,

> last
>
> fast

and move to alternating rhyme,

> last
>
> fast
>
> bring
>
> search
>
> sing
>
> birch

you would DECELERATE the system.

Of course, if you kept going with alternating rhyme in the first case, and with consecutive rhyme in the second case, the PACE for both sections would be CONSTANT.

EXERCISE 22: ACCELERATE THE FOLLOWING LISTS BY ADDING OR SUBTRACTING WORDS. TRY TO FIND RHYMES THAT MAKE SENSE WITH THE WORDS ALREADY THERE. THEN, START OVER AND DECELERATE THEM.

ACCELERATE:

1. niece
   stumble
   fleece

2. decide
   ride
   course

3. fulfill
   returning
   unlock

DECELERATE:

1. niece
   stumble
   fleece

2. decide
   ride
   course

3. fulfill
   returning
   unlock

As you can see in number two, once you have consecutive rhymes, the pedal is to the metal. You cannot accelerate. The only way to go faster then is to shorten PHRASE LENGTHS. In juggling, when the balls are going at top speed, the only way to juggle faster is to *decrease the distance* the balls have to go.

III. FLOW

I watched a juggler once who really impressed me. He juggled four balls, faster and faster. Suddenly he stopped and announced that he was about to juggle counter-clockwise, which he did. After a while he stopped again and announced that he would juggle first clockwise and then counter-clockwise without stopping. Our job was to try to tell where he changed. It was like magic. I really couldn't tell. Things looked a little funny for just a second, and then it dawned on me that the balls were moving counter-clockwise. The transformation had been practically seamless.

Sometimes you will want seamless transformations from idea to idea. Sometimes you will want to stop and start over again. You can do this, even inside a lyric section, by making your rhymes stop or by making them push ahead. Rhyme is the best way to control a lyric's FLOW. Nothing can match rhyme's power in this area. Not phrase length. Not rhythm. This moves by starts and stops:

> Had we but world enough and time
>
> This coyness, lady, were no crime . . .
>
> An hundred years should go to praise
>
> Thine eyes, and on thy forehead gaze;
>
> Two hundred to adore each breast,
>
> And thirty thousand to the rest; . . .
>
> But at my back I always hear
>
> Time's winged chariot hurrying near . . .
>
> —Andrew Marvell, from "To His Coy Mistress"

Even in 1681 poets were smooth talking sweet young things. (Rod Stewart singing "Tonight's the Night" comes to mind, among many others.) Marvell's lines are 8-syllable, 4-stress (tetrameter) couplets. Each rhymed couplet works as a little unit of thought, almost like a paragraph. Each couplet rhymes and stops the motion, interrupting the FLOW of the poem. Equal length lines create balanced couplets, but it is rhyme that applies the brakes.

Watch how this one moves:

> . . . And on the pedestal these words appear:
>
> "My name is Ozymandias, king of kings:
>
> Look on my works, ye Mighty, and despair!"
>
> Nothing beside remains. Round the decay
>
> Of that colossal wreck, boundless and bare
>
> The lone and level sands stretch far away.
>
> —Percy Bysshe Shelly, from "Ozymandias"

The rhyme scheme for these last six lines of "Ozymandius" is

appear	a
kings	b
despair	a (imperfect rhyme)
decay	c
bare	a
away	c

"Kings" rhymes with "things" three lines earlier. "Appear" is an imperfect rhyme (technically, a Consonance Rhyme) with "despair" and "bare." This little rhyme system is seamless. It continues without hesitation all the way to the end. In its fourth line, it would have closed if it had used either "things" or "bare:"

appear	a		appear	a
kings	b		kings	b
despair	a		despair	a
things	b		bare	a
decay	c		decay	c
away	c		away	c

Either way, the six line system would have FRAGMENTED, it would have had an *internal point of closure*. Instead, at line four a new sound (long ā in "decay") keeps it moving, so the system is THROUGH-WRITTEN.

The simplest paradigm for a THROUGH-WRITTEN system is, like rhythm Paradigm One:

a
b
a
b

The simplest paradigm for a FRAGMENTED system is, like rhythm Paradigm Two:

a
a
b
b

The "a's" "bond" together to cause a point of rest or resolution inside the aabb structure. For the same reason,

a
a
b

is also FRAGMENTED. The "a's" again form a bond, just as they did before. Whether or not another sound comes afterwards makes no difference. The balancing has already happened.

There is a strong relationship between FLOW and CLOSURE, since a FRAGMENTED system CLOSES internally, and a THROUGH-WRITTEN system remains OPEN internally. We might even say that the FRAGMENTED system

a
a
b
b

is two smaller systems:

> a
> a
>
> and
>
> b
> b

Usually we call a a b b one or two systems depending on their content, not on their structure. If we decide to call it one system, we would call it FRAGMENTED, or internally closed. If we decide to call it two systems it would be two smaller THROUGH-WRITTEN systems.

Much of the time, consecutive rhymes fragment a system.

> a   a   a   a
> a   a   a   a
> a   b   b   b
>   b   c

But the following are not fragmented:

> a   a
> b   b
> b   a
>   c
>   c

These do not fragment because the consecutive rhymes come *after* elements that create some stronger effect. In the first case, there is an odd number of phrases. In the second case you are looking for a resolution of "b," plus an even number of phrases; "c c" is just a delay.

EXERCISE 23: PUT A "T" FOR "THROUGH-WRITTEN" OR "F" FOR FRAGMENTED IN EACH BLANK. THEN, SUBSTITUTE WORDS FOR LETTERS IN EACH EXAMPLE. CHOOSE TWO OF YOUR RESULTS, ONE THROUGH-WRITTEN AND ONE FRAGMENTED, AND WRITE COMPLETE PHRASES. GROUP YOUR IDEAS ACCORDING TO THE FLOW OF THE RHYME SCHEME.

1. ____ a b a b: 1. THROUGH-WRITTEN:

2. ____ a a b b:

3. ____ a a a b:

4. ____ a b b a:

5. ____ a a a:

6. ____ a a b a: 2. FRAGMENTED

7. ____ a b b a a:

8. ____ a b a a:

9. ____ a b a a b:

10. ____ a b a b a:

answers: 1. T; 2. F; 3. F; 4. T; 5. F; 6. F; 7. T; 8. T; 9. F; 10. F

IV. CLOSURE

I have been trying to come up with an easy way of saying what makes a system close (or resolve). Part of it is simple. If a system is balanced, it is closed. It would be nice if that was all there was to it. But alas, some systems that are not balanced are nonetheless closed. For example,

a	bank
b	loan
a	rank
c	nerve
c	serve
b	throne

is closed, but it is also unbalanced. I thought the best way to handle these situations would be to look at some systems that are unbalanced and closed, and say why they are closed.

Start with the example above. It is closed because it has an even number of phrases, each piece is partnered off, and its main system,

a

b

a

⋮

b

although interrupted by the acceleration

c

c

is closed. It is the acceleration that makes it unbalanced.

Here is another system.

a	bank
b	loan
a	rank
b	throne
c	nerve
c	serve

This is closed because it is a FRAGMENTED system containing two BALANCED parts. Anytime you see something like this, you will know that the system is closed.

Other systems may be closed and unbalanced because they are DECEPTIVE or UNEXPECTED closures. We will look at them shortly. These systems are OPEN:

a	a
b	a
a	a
c	b
c	b

Both systems need another member to close them.

EXERCISE 24: PUT C FOR CLOSED OR O FOR OPEN IN EACH BLANK. THEN, SUBSTITUTE WORDS FOR LETTERS.

1. ____ a b a b a

2. ____ a a b b b

3. ____ a a a b b

4. ____ a b c a b

5. ____ a b c a c

6. ____ a b b a

7. ____ a b b a a

8. ____ a b b a b b

9. ____ a b c c b

10. ____ a a b

NOW, CHOOSE TWO OF YOUR ANSWERS, ONE OPEN AND ONE CLOSED, AND WRITE SECTIONS FOR THEM. MAKE THE LENGTHS AND RHYTHMS OF PHRASES FOLLOW THE RHYME SCHEME: WHERE RHYME SOUNDS MATCH, MAKE YOUR PHRASES AND RHYTHMS MATCH. WHEN RHYME SOUNDS CHANGE, USE DIFFERENT PHRASE LENGTHS AND RHYTHMS.

1. CLOSED:

2. OPEN:

V. TYPES OF CLOSURE

When a rhyme system is CLOSED, it sometimes closes in an abnormal way. Sometimes it sets you up to expect certain things:

fool

slow

school . . .

sets you up for

fool

slow

school

low

to close the system. Call it EXPECTED CLOSURE whenever the system delivers what you expect. But you can close systems in another way:

fool	a
slow	b
school	a
rule	a

Call this a DECEPTIVE closure. Even when the system is lengthened, maybe by an acceleration,

fool

slow

school

nitwit

sit . . .

you still expect

low

In the system above, you have two possible DECEPTIONS:

fool	a		fool	a
slow	b		slow	b
school	a		school	a
nitwit	c		nitwit	c
sit	c		sit	c
rule	a		spit	c

both are DECEPTIVE.

As you have already seen in the chapter on RHYTHM, there are two conditions for a CLOSURE to be DECEPTIVE,

1. The system must raise expectations that it will be resolved in a certain way, and
2. The phrase that is actually used to resolve the system must already be in the structure. Now look at

fool	a
slow	b
school	a
rise	c

and,

fool	a
school	a
sow	b
slip	c

Neither one is DECEPTIVE. They are both OPEN. In the place you expect the closure they do not use a sound used already in the system.

A resolution is UNEXPECTED in either of two cases:

1. where your expectations have already been satisfied, and the last sound you used is repeated, as in

blood	a	blood	a
flood	a	crash	b
crash	b	flood	a
bash	b	bash	b
mash	b	mash	b

Sometimes this UNEXPECTED CLOSURE is a little iffy.

a	a
a	b
a	a
	b
	a

These could be closed, or maybe open. It seems to depend on what the last "a" is doing there. Is it starting something new, or adding to something old? Is it looking backward or forward? In

> You're breaking me in two
>
> Why can't I have you?
>
> Why can't I have you?

it is clear that we are looking backward. It is a pretty clear case of Identity. When the third "a" repeats like this, I think the system really has only two phrases. So it is closed. But if this happens,

> You're breaking me in two
>
> Why can't you be true?
>
> Why can't I have you?

the odd number of phrases comes into play more and you notice the need for another phrase. Repitition of rhymes "aaa" plays against balance, and leaves the CLOSURE ambiguous. The same reasoning applies to the longer system, "a b a b a." Both of these systems seem more OPEN than CLOSED. Both systems are good ways to leave your listener in a little cloud of mystery. Do not be upset by ambiguity. A little bit is a very useful thing.

2. Resolution is also expected when the system sets up no clear expectations before the resolution, as in

fool	a
slow	b
rise	c
surprise	c

Even Shakespeare is fond of this one. He likes to use it when he wants to get out of an unrhymed section of Blank Verse (unrhymed iambic pentameter lines). This example from *Othello* will do:

Emilia:	. . . Let husbands know
	Their wives have sense like them: they see and smell
	And have their palates both for sweet and sour,
	As husbands have. . . . And have not we affections
	Desires for sport, and frailty, as men have?
	Then let them use us well: else let them know
	The ills we do, their ills instruct us so.

OTHELLO. Act IV, scene iii. 94–104

Sting can do it too.

Be still my broken dreams	x
Shattered like a fallen glass	x
I'm not ready to be broken just *yet*	*a*
A lesson just learned is so hard to for*get*	*a*

This closure comes out of nowhere. It is a real surprise. If you put important or surprising ideas in spots where the structure surprises, the ideas will work with the structure to create lovely PROSODY.

Here is an example you saw earlier. It uses a DECEPTIVE CLOSURE at phrase four, and then adds an UNEXPECTED CLOSURE at phrase five. The title is "SHE'LL PUT YOU ON THE ROPES."

SHE'LL PUT YOU ON THE ROPES	a
She likes to get her kicks	b
She'll take you by the throat	a
Strangle all your hopes	a
SHE'LL PUT YOU ON THE ROPES	a

Spotlights blaze at the closing phrase, which just happens to be the title. Whether a CLOSURE is DECEPTIVE or UNEXPECTED, it turns on attention-getting spotlights.

EXERCISE 25: PUT E FOR EXPECTED, U FOR UNEXPECTED, OR D FOR DECEPTIVE IN EACH OF THE BLANKS PROVIDED. THEN, SUBSTITUTE WORDS FOR THE LETTERS IN EACH RHYME SCHEME.

1. ____ a b a b b

2. ____ a b a a

3. ____ a a b b a

4. ____ a a b a

5. ____ a b a a a

6. ____ a b a c c a

7. ____ a b a c c b

8 ____ a b a a b

9. ____ a a a

10. ____ a b c a a a

answers: 1. U; 2. D; 3. U; 4. D; 5. D; 6. U & D; 7. E; 8. D & U; 9. U; 10. D

EXERCISE 26: WRITE A LYRIC SECTION WITH A DECEPTIVE RHYME CLOSURE USING PARA-DIGM THREE FROM CHAPTER 3 FOR ITS RHYTHM. THEN WRITE A LYRIC SECTION WITH AN UN-EXPECTED RHYME CLOSURE. EITHER ADD AN EXTRA PHRASE AFTER IT IS CLOSED, OR RHYME IT FOR THE FIRST TIME AT THE END.

DECEPTIVE:

UNEXPECTED:

You have now seen the "What." You can move on to "Why." Time to start juggling.

RHYME STRATEGIES

Once you understand the effect that rhyme structure has on a system, you can start to develop strategies for choosing them. There are three basic rhyme strategies:

1. Outlining the way ideas move.
2. Supporting meaning. (Prosody)
3. Creating relationships between sections.

1. *Outlining the way ideas move.*

The movement of your lyric's ideas can be outlined and supported by your rhyme scheme. As you have seen, there is a big difference between these two rhyme schemes:

a	a
a	b
b	a
b	b

An a a b b rhyme scheme divides the structure into two parts. The division suggests a parallel division of ideas: one idea for a a, the other for b b.

a)	Love her or leave her to me	a
	Keep her or let her go free	a
	Don't go two-timing her	b
	'less you're resignin' her	b

On the other hand, abab is THROUGH-WRITTEN. It keeps the system and the idea moving.

b)	Some girls like their flirtin'	a
	They're always on the roam	b
	Blind to who they're hurtin'	a
	Their eyes are never home	b

Another way of stating this first strategy: when you want ideas to flow, through-write the rhyme scheme; when you want ideas to "section off," fragment it.

EXERCISE 27: KEEPING AS MUCH OF THE SAME MEANING AS POSSIBLE, REWRITE A) AND B) TO GET THE OPPOSITE EFFECTS: THROUGH-WRITE A) AND FRAGMENT B). (YOU MAY WANT TO LENGTHEN OR SHORTEN SOME OF THE PHRASES.)

REWRITE OF A): (LOVE HER OR LEAVE HER TO ME)

REWRITE OF B): (SOME GIRLS LIKE THEIR FLIRTIN')

2. *Supporting meaning (Prosody).*

Another important reason to choose a strategy is Prosody: making the rhyme system work with its *content*. Look again at this:

VERSE	If I went into analysis	a
	And took myself apart	b
	And laid me out for both of us to see	c
	You'd go into paralysis	a
	Right there in my arms	b
	Finding out you're not a bit like me	c
CHORUS	READY OR NOT	d
	We've got what we've got	d
	Let's give it a shot	d
	READY OR NOT	d

The verse rhymes are spread apart. Their leisurely pace works pretty well with the idea, especially for the first three phrases. As the rhymes start to connect the last three phrases to the first three, the pressure pushes the section forward. The chorus rhymes are consecutive, one after another (as fast as rhymes can go). They are ideal for the "out-of-the-starting-blocks" idea of the chorus.

As above, Prosody is used to contrast different sections (in this case, verse and chorus), but it can also support the way ideas move within a section. If you are working with an idea that gets more active or more intense as it develops, consider accelerating the rhyme scheme:

I saw her once and that was it	a
I felt my knees go weak	b
I tossed and turned all night in bed	c
Knew she had me in her web	c
Tried to make her leave my head	c
Couldn't fall asleep	b

The consecutive rhymes in lines 3, 4, and 5 accelerate the section and build pressure, working in sync with the idea. The same scheme is used below for the same effect, this time with some feminine rhymes to heighten the comedy:

d)	You can't play ping pong with my heart	a
	When I'm without a paddle	b
	It's 40-love, you've got the ball	c
	The odds are astronomical	c
	The situation's comical	c
	You've really got me rattled	b

Usually you start with an *idea* and *develop* a rhyme scheme to suit it. This seems like the most natural way. It is the way I worked out both a) and b) above. Other times you have to start with your *rhyme scheme* and develop with an idea that *fits it*. This is not as unusual as it sounds. Almost every lyric you write will have at least two verses. By the time you have written verse 1, you have decided on a rhyme scheme. You will usually repeat the same rhyme scheme in the next verse, so you will need to work out an idea to fit the rhyme scheme you already have.

d1)   You can't play ping pong with my heart   a
       When I'm without a paddle   b
       It's 20-love, you've got the ball   c
       The odds are astronomical   c
       The situation's comical   c
       You've really got me rattled   b

d2)   You can't play ping pong with my heart   a
       You dominate the table   d
       My nerves are shot, you've won the set   e
       Your curves have got me in a sweat   e
       My vision's blurred, can't see the net   e
       I'm feeling most unstable   d

The rhyme scheme is the same, and the ideas move to fit it. The phrase lengths work with the ideas and the rhyme scheme.

EXERCISE 28: TRY WORKING FROM RHYME SCHEME TO IDEAS. FOR EACH OF THE RHYME SCHEMES BELOW, THINK UP A PLOT WHOSE ACTION FITS THE MOVEMENT OF THE RHYME SCHEME. THEN, COME UP WITH RHYME WORDS FOR YOUR PLOT. HERE IS AN EXAMPLE:

RHYME SCHEME: A B A C C B

PLOT SKETCH:

>   My lover and I are dancing, enjoying our closeness.
>   My spouse enters the lounge and spots me. We have been
>   discovered!

Rhyme words: dance/embrace/romance/eyes/surprise/disgrace

Your turn.

1. RHYME SCHEME: A A B B C C

   PLOT SKETCH:

   RHYME WORDS:

2. RHYME SCHEME: X A X A B B

   PLOT SKETCH:

   RHYME WORDS:

3. RHYME SCHEME: A A B C C C

   PLOT SKETCH:

   RHYME WORDS:

Prosody is one of the most important strategies you have, but remember: whenever you write a section whose structure will be repeated, design your prosody carefully. Think ahead to the next section too. Will your structure fit the next idea too? Look again at c:

c)	I saw her once and that was it	a
	I felt my knees go weak	b
	I tossed and turned all night in bed	c
	Knew she had me in her web	c
	Tried to make her leave my head	c
	Couldn't fall asleep	b

What if the idea for the next section went something like:

"After I got to know her, she became a good friend rather

than a lover or captor. The time we spent together was

some of the most relaxing I've had."

Now the rhyme scheme will not work, because it builds too much excitement late in the structure for the way the new idea develops. You are in trouble. You could try to:

i. Change the rhyme scheme to compromise between the two ideas.

c)	I saw her once and that was it	a
	I felt my knees go weak	b
	I tossed and turned all night long in bed	c
	Oooo she really gave me fits	a
	Couldn't fall asleep	b
	Though I tried, she wouldn't leave my head	c

ii. Come up with a different developmental idea to match the original rhyme scheme better.

iii. Keep the Verse rhyme scheme the same, and use the "relaxation" idea (if you really are married to it) as a Bridge section so you do not have to repeat the old rhyme scheme with the new idea. Of course you probably will still have to come up with another idea to match the old rhyme scheme. The final strategy for choosing a rhyme scheme is:

3. *To create relationships between sections.*

Should a particular section move forward or should it stop? How strong should the push forward or the stop be? How strong should the contrast be between sections? This third strategy will be easier to deal with after the next chapter on FORMAL ELEMENTS. Let us turn to it now.

CHAPTER FIVE
FORM: TOSSING THE BALLS TOGETHER

Lyrics are made up of pieces: syllables gather into words, words form phrases and phrases stack up into sections, sections group into *"song systems,"* which finally work together to create the lyric. A lyric is like a piece of music, it moves forward one syllable at a time, *through* time. It is not like a painting, which you can experience all at once. Lyric structure is your guide on this forward journey. The easiest way to understand the journey is to keep two simple ideas in mind: MOVING and STOPPING. You can look at the job of each lyric section in terms of one or the other.

Until now I have asked you to build only lyric sections. In this chapter you will link sections together to form larger groups. Start by thinking of each lyric section as either a CENTRAL SECTION or a DEVELOPMENTAL SECTION. Everything within the lyric *moves toward or departs from* a CENTRAL SECTION. Like ancient Rome, all roads lead to a CENTRAL SECTION and every other place is just a stop along the way.

The CENTRAL SECTION should contain the CENTRAL IDEA, or main point, of the lyric. The CENTRAL *SECTION* is the structural *centerpiece* of the lyric. The CENTRAL *IDEA* is the main message of the lyric. Put them together.

DEVELOPMENTAL SECTIONS contain DEVELOPMENTAL IDEAS: ideas that *lead up to* or *develop* the CENTRAL IDEA. They should move forward until they get to a CENTRAL SECTION. You, of course, have to decide what you want your lyric to say — what your CENTRAL IDEA will be. Once you have decided, construct a CENTRAL SECTION for it. Then construct your DEVELOPMENTAL SECTIONS to serve THE CENTRAL SECTION. Each section in your lyric will have its own job to do. Here are the most typical jobs, so typical that they have names:

> VERSE
>
> CHORUS
>
> BRIDGE
>
> REFRAIN
>
> HOOK

A lyric does not have to have all these elements to work properly. A clock doesn't have to have an alarm to keep time.

SONG ELEMENTS
Verse

The Verse is the basic worker of the lyric. Its jobs are

1. To introduce ideas
2. To set up the CENTRAL IDEA
3. To develop or continue ideas
4. To set structural standards for the lyric,

thus, 5. Verses should close down.

The first three deal with idea development, a subject for another whole book. For now let's concentrate on verse *structure*.

Verses set structural standards for the lyric

Verses establish BALANCE, PACE, FLOW, CLOSURE, AND CLOSURE TYPE for the lyric, setting a point of comparison for other structures in the lyric. Verses establish your expectations for the lyric, much like a juggler who establishes a pattern so he can surprise you with variations. Here is an example of a verse.

The carousel spun smooth as glass

Those childhood summer nights

I spent my time for rings of brass

Beneath the sparkling lights

The common meter and a b a b rhyme scheme come through clearly. The section closes down just as you expect it to. Now you are set up: you have a point of reference for recognizing either repetition or contrast.

The rings came easy to my hand

My parents stood and smiled

They fell to me at my command

A golden summer's child

With the first Verse as a reference point, it is easy to recognize this as repetition — as another Verse. It is just as easy to hear the contrast in this section:

One by one we reach for the chances

One by one we move down the line

Day by year in smooth revolving dances

One by one we sail away out of time

Although the new section maintains the a b a b rhyme scheme, its phrases are longer.

One by one we reach for the chances

One by one we move down the line

Day by year in smooth revolving dances

One by one we sail away out of time

This section has longer phrases. Longer than what? Longer than the verses. It will require a different musical treatment than the verses. It also seems to sum up or comment on the verse information. The verses set up, then serve this new section. It is the CENTRAL SECTION, and contains the CENTRAL IDEA, in this case, life's passage through time.

Sometimes a verse itself contains the CENTRAL IDEA. When it does, it is usually a CENTRAL SECTION.

When I was seventeen IT WAS A VERY GOOD YEAR

IT WAS A VERY GOOD YEAR for small town girls

On soft summer nights

We'd hide from the lights

On the village green

When I was seventeen

        — Ervin Drake, "IT WAS A VERY GOOD YEAR"

Again, the verse sets the standard. Again, it is easy to recognize a repetition:

When I was twenty-one IT WAS A VERY GOOD YEAR

IT WAS A VERY GOOD YEAR for city girls

Who lived up the stair

With perfumed hair

That came undone

When I was twenty-one

"IT WAS A VERY GOOD YEAR," like many songs, is made up only of verses. It has no contrasting sections. When you write a lyric that contains only verses, make sure they are interesting.

> When I was thirty-five IT WAS A VERY GOOD YEAR
>
> IT WAS A VERY GOOD YEAR for blue-blooded girls
>
> Of independent means
>
> We'd ride in limousines
>
> Their chauffeurs would drive
>
> When I was thirty five

In the fourth verse there is a wonderful variation. You expect the CENTRAL IDEA to be the second phrase because that's where it was in the other verses. But no.

> But now the days are short, I'm in the autumn of the year
>
> And now I think of my life as a vintage wine
>
> From fine old kegs
>
> From the brim to the dregs
>
> It poured sweet and clear
>
> IT WAS A VERY GOOD YEAR

Saving the CENTRAL IDEA till last has two effects:

1. It calls attention to the *second* phrase, which contains an important idea.

2. It takes you by surprise. Whole flotillas of spotlights turn on to light up the CENTRAL IDEA.

The thing I like best about this lyric is the double meaning in "IT WAS A VERY GOOD YEAR" that is set up by

> And now I think of my life as a vintage wine
>
> From fine old kegs . . .

Lovely work.

Verses should work like the paragraphs of an essay, moving forward from one idea to the next. Look carefully at "IT WAS A VERY GOOD YEAR." Each verse moves to a new place.

Chorus

1. Completes, comments on, or summarizes ideas.
2. Contains the CENTRAL IDEA.
3. Is the lyric's CENTRAL SECTION.
4. Is typically the lyric's most balanced section.
thus, 5. Stops forward motion.

Because every song that has a Chorus has one or more verses, a Chorus is usually a contrasting element. The verse ideas move toward or "come home" to the Chorus. Because the Chorus is a CENTRAL SECTION — *a place where ideas are completed* — the end of the Chorus should *stop forward motion.* This creates the feeling of "starting over again" in the next section. Here is an excellent Chorus.

> And I let time go by so slow
>
> And I made every moment last
>
> And I thought about YEARS
>
> How they take so long
>
> And they go so fast

This certainly fits all five of the prescriptions for a Chorus. It summarizes and comments on the verses. It contains the CENTRAL IDEA: "Years are both fast and slow at the same time." It is the lyric's CENTRAL ELEMENT, in terms of structure and meaning, it is *the most balanced element in the lyric*, and it stops motion. Of course, as you saw earlier, it does its own trick with phrase lengths. Being *most* balanced doesn't necessarily mean *perfectly* balanced.

Beth Nielsen Chapman also does a neat trick with stresses to balance the section. The first two phrases are three stresses (2 x 3 = 6):

> And I let time go by so slow
> And I made every moment last

The last three phrases are each two stresses (3 x 2 = 6):

> And I thought about Years
> How they take so long
> And they go so fast

A balancing act with built in acceleration.

The verse phrases are long. It takes a long time to get from rhyme to rhyme. It is even a challenge to figure out exactly where some of the phrases start and stop. And the "just-barely-if-at-all" rhyme "there/year" sort of trails off as you watch the singer look around and remember. . .

> Across the street
>> the Randall's oldest daughter must have come home
> Her two boys built a snowman by the backyard swings
> I thought of Old Man Randall and his Christmas decorations
> And how he used to leave them up till early spring
> And I thought of all the summers
> I paced that porch and swore I'd die of boredom there
> And I thought of what I'd give
>> to feel another summer linger when a day feels like a year

Then into the Chorus. Neat.

Song System

Either I made up this name, or my friend Tom Frazee did. I don't remember which. A "Song System" is a group of sections that work together in larger movements, or cycles of motion. The idea is especially helpful when looking at a group of contrasting sections.

A Song System always has a CENTRAL SECTION and often has one or more DEVELOP-MENTAL SECTIONS. For example, if a lyric has

> verse
>
> Chorus
>
> verse
>
> Chorus

it has 2 Song Systems:

> S1. verse/Chorus
>
> S2. verse/Chorus

Each Song System is a cycle. Each closes down after the CENTRAL SECTION. Once you finish a Song System, you have to start something else: maybe another system just like the one you finished, or maybe something different. But one thing is clear: you have finished something, so you must either be through with the song, or start something up again.

The verse and Chorus of "Years" is a Song System. So is this:

When I left I left walking wounded   VERSE
I made my escape from the rain
Still a prisoner of hurt
I had months worth of work
Freeing my mind of the pain
I had hours of sitting alone in the dark
Listening to sad songs and coming apart
Lord knows I made crying an art
Weak is a SLOW HEALING HEART

A SLOW HEALING HEART   CHORUS
Is dying to mend
Longing for love
Lonely again
When a spirit is broken
And the memories start
Nothing moves slower
Than A SLOW HEALING HEART

— Jim Rushing, "SLOW HEALING HEART"

Talking about Song Systems is the most useful in lyrics that have different kinds of sections: Verse + Chorus, Verse + Bridge + Chorus, Bridge + Chorus. Song Systems give you a way to describe how larger units (groups or sections) work together. It comes in handy.

In a lyric where all the sections are the same, and each section contains the CENTRAL IDEA ("IT WAS A VERY GOOD YEAR," for example), the concept of Song System doesn't help much. You could talk about "sections" just as easily.

Bridge

This section is often called a "release," or boredom breaker: the place where you try to get away from the ideas and structures the lyric has already established. But it is also much more:

1. It is a DEVELOPMENTAL section.
2. It develops a new perspective or contrasting idea.
3. It unbalances the section by moving away from established structures, creating structural tension.
4. It is resolved by a return to previously established structures,

thus, 5. It is frequently the lyric's most unbalanced section.

THE GREAT PRETENDER

O yes I'm THE GREAT PRETENDER
Pretending that I'm doing well
My need is such
I pretend too much
I'm lonely but no one can tell

O yes I'm THE GREAT PRETENDER
Adrift in a world of my own
I play the game

But to my real shame
You've left me to dream all alone

    Too real is this feeling of make believe
    Too real when I feel what my heart can't conceal

Yes I'm THE GREAT PRETENDER
Just laughing and gay like a clown
I seem to be
What I'm not, you see
I'm wearing my heart like a crown
Pretending that you're still around

A very pretty bridge. Though it feels like a section, it still throws you off balance a little, which gets you ready to move into the last verse. Look.

Too real is this feeling of make believe
Too real when I feel what my heart can't conceal

One ball moves smoothly: the *rhythm* is balanced and gives you a nice feeling of section. But one ball is unbalanced. You want to hear a rhyme with "believe:"

Too real is this feeling of make be*lieve*	a
Too real when I feel what my heart can't con*ceive*	a

But what you get is:

Too *real* is this *feel*ing of make believe	a
Too *real* when I *feel* what my heart can't con*ceal*	b

A slick deception that throws you off balance with *five* "eel" sounds. Since you are a little off balance, the return to familiar territory is a relief. A new and bigger Song System is formed.

> Too real is this feeling of make believe
> Too real when I feel what my heart can't conceal
>
> Yes I'm THE GREAT PRETENDER
> Just laughing and gay like a clown
> I seem to be
> What I'm not, you see
> I'm wearing my heart like a crown
> Pretending that you're still around

An A A B A song form is effective partly because it creates this sense of resolution when it moves back to the third verse. The structure of the first two verses defines "home base." Then, the Bridge takes you away from home — away from the verse structure. So when you come back to the third verse, you come back home to familiar territory. It is a real homecoming, like seeing the old neighborhood again after a long trip. The tension created by moving away has been resolved.
This last Song System is made up of

(Bridge   →   Verse),
or
(DEVELOPMENTAL SECTION   →   CENTRAL SECTION).

The sense of arrival when you get to the third verse is the same thing you feel when you move to the Chorus in a Verse/Chorus Song System. A new Song System is formed by the DEVELOP-MENTAL SECTION moving into the CENTRAL SECTION.

Here's another one.

THESE ARE THE DAYS

THESE ARE THE DAYS of apple wine

THESE ARE THE DAYS so sweet and clear

This is the time we've waited for all our lives

THESE ARE THE DAYS rare

THESE ARE THE DAYS of grace and age

THESE ARE THE DAYS for harvesting

This is the time to gather the songs we've saved

THESE ARE THE DAYS to sing

> And so September's here at last
>
> I can't believe it's come so fast
>
> Sweet and bitter, now the season's ripe
>
> Here together, all the rest behind

THESE ARE THE DAYS for drinking deep

THESE ARE THE DAYS for growing bold

This is the time of warmth before winter's sleep

THESE ARE THE DAYS of gold

In this Bridge the rhyme scheme is balanced but the phrase lengths shorten. The rhyme scheme is interesting. It is either

And so September's here at last	a
I can't believe it's come so fast	a
Sweet and bitter, now the season's ripe	b
Here together, all the rest behind	b

or maybe, if you hear the weak syllable rhyme "ter/ther,"

And so September's here at last	a
I can't believe it's come so fast	a
Sweet and bitter	b
Now the season's ripe	c
Here together	b
Leave the rest behind	c

Either way, a section is formed. The shorter phrases near the end accelerate the section and throw it slightly off balance.

A bridge works exactly the same way when *it is inserted AFTER TWO COMPLETE SONG SYSTEMS IN A VERSE/CHORUS LYRIC*. In this case each verse/chorus system, because it functions as a complete unit, works like a verse section in an A A B A form. Here is a fine example by Donald Fagen and Walter Becker of Steely Dan:

HAITIAN DIVORCE

Song System 1:

Babs and Clean Willie were in love they said	VERSE
So in love the preacher's face turned red	
Soon everybody knew the thing was dead	
He shouts, she bites	
They wrangle through the night	
She go crazy	
Gotta make a getaway	
Papa say	

O, No Hesitation	CHORUS
No tears and no hearts breaking	
No remorse	
O, Congratulations!	
This is your HAITIAN DIVORCE	

Song System 2:

She takes the taxi to the good hotel	VERSE
Bon marché, as far as she can tell	
She drinks the zombie from the cocoa shell	
She feels allright	
She get it on tonight	
Mister driver	
Take me where the music play	
Papa say	

O, No Hesitation	CHORUS
No tears and no hearts breaking	
No remorse	
O, Congratulations!	
This is your HAITIAN DIVORCE	

Song System 3:

At the Grotto	BRIDGE
In the greasy chair	
Sits the Charlie with the lotion	
And the kinky hair	
When she smiled she said it all	
The band was hot so	
They danced the famous merango	
Now we dolly back	
Now we fade to black	

Tearful reunion in the U.S.A.	VERSE
Day by day those memories fade away	
Some babies grow in a peculiar way	
It changed, it grew	
Then everybody knew	
Semi-mojo	
Who's this kinky so-and-so	
Papa go	
O, No Hesitation	CHORUS
No tears and no hearts breaking	
No remorse	
O, Congratulations!	
This is your HAITIAN DIVORCE	

The Bridge makes a clear move away from the structures of the Verse and Chorus.

At the Grotto	a
In the greasy chair	b
Sits the Charlie with the lotion	c
And the kinky hair . . .	b

In this lyric, the Bridge leads to another verse. As long as the bridge takes you back to familiar territory, the sense of return or resolution will be there. The Bridge re-focuses attention from Papa and Babs onto

the Charlie with the lotion

And the kinky hair

This is a new twist, a plot thickener. There is also a grand sweep of time and space.

Now we dolly back

Now we fade to black

All these new ideas, plus the new phrase lengths and a new rhyme scheme are a real trip away from home base, making the return to the verse a homecoming, where there is, appropriately enough, a

Tearful reunion in the U.S.A.

Home at last.

Transitional Bridge

This is as close as I can come to an accurate name for this elusive little section. I have heard it called by many names:

Pre-Chorus	Vest	Ramp
Climb or Lift	Verse Extension	Prime

This section is used for so many jobs, none of these descriptive names quite fit all of them:

1. It is a DEVELOPMENTAL section.
2. It introduces a pivotal idea as a transition between Verse and Chorus.
3. It is always enclosed in a Song System, almost always between a verse and a chorus.

4. It unbalances the Song System by contrasting with the established verse structure. It makes you want to get to a balanced or CENTRAL section.

Thus,   5. It is usually the lyric's shortest and most unbalanced section.

A quick example. This one by Ric Ocasek of The Cars is typical:

WHY CAN'T I HAVE YOU

Song System 1:

Dreamy lips, set in motion, flashing	VERSE
Breathless hush, pounding soft, lasting	
Glossy mouth, taste untamed, moving	
Carousel, up and down	
Just like you	
Just one more time to touch you	TR. BR.
Just one more time to tell you	
You're on my mind	
WHY CAN'T I HAVE YOU	CHORUS
You're breaking my heart in two	
You know what I'm going through	
WHY CAN'T I HAVE YOU	

The structure of this Transitional Bridge is VERY effective. Its first two lines don't rhyme, but they make a couplet with repeating rhythmic structure:

Just one more time to touch you

Just one more time to tell you

The third line is short, unbalancing the section both in length and with an odd number of phrases.

Just one more time to touch you

Just one more time to tell you

You're on my mind

Added to these unbalancing techniques is the imperfect rhyme "time/mind" positioned to trip you up like a piano wire stretched across the road:

Just one more time to touch you

Just one more time to tell you

You're on my mind

WHY CAN'T I HAVE YOU

You're breaking my heart in two

You know what I'm going through

WHY CAN'T I HAVE YOU

Not only does this asymmetrical position push you forward, but it sets you up for the long "ī" sound of the key words of the HOOK: "*WHY* CAN'T *I* HAVE YOU"! The chorus "ī" sounds are also positioned asymmetrically, so there is no resolution until the end of the system.

The second Transitional Bridge in this lyric uses the same technique, but changes the words in the third phrase:

Song System 2:

Candy smile, all the while, glinting	VERSE
Your eyes like mica, lethal pout, hinting	
Felt the pressure tight and warm, softly striking	
I tripped and stumbled, I cling forever	
I go all night	
Just one more time to touch you	TR. BR.
Just one more time to tell you	
I'm not so blind	
WHY CAN'T I HAVE YOU ...	CHORUS

A Transitional Bridge can change. Here, one phrase makes a difference in meaning, but the structure is preserved. The tripping effect at the long "i" rhyme at "blind" again sets up the sound of the Title. You won't use Transitional Bridges too often unless you write dance songs, in R&B and more Pop-oriented rock, where songs rely on a strong dance groove. Both verse and chorus usually have the same groove, so a Transitional Bridge is inserted between them as a "release" — to break the monotony and build tension for a return to the groove. In this way, a Transitional Bridge works just like a typical Bridge. But remember, a Transitional Bridge comes *before* the Song System has closed down, *between* a Verse and a Chorus. The more typical Bridge always comes *after* a song system has closed down.

Refrain

This is not a section at all. It is just a name for the part of a *Verse* that contains the CENTRAL IDEA and gets repeated in the other Verses. A Refrain is different from a Chorus, since a Chorus is contained in *its own separate section*. "Refrain" is a handy term when you talk about lyrics that have only Verses, or Verses and a Bridge. These verses have a Refrain:

{ *O yes I'm THE GREAT PRETENDER* }

Pretending that I'm doing well

My need is such

I pretend too much

I'm lonely but no one can tell

{ *O yes I'm THE GREAT PRETENDER* }

Adrift in a world of my own

I play the game

But to my real shame

You've left me to dream all alone

— Buck Ram "THE GREAT PRETENDER"

And this:

When I was seventeen *IT WAS A VERY GOOD YEAR*

IT WAS A VERY GOOD YEAR for small town girls

And soft summer nights

We'd hide from the lights

On the village green

When I was seventeen

When I was twenty-one *IT WAS A VERY GOOD YEAR*

IT WAS A VERY GOOD YEAR for city girls

Who lived up the stair

With perfumed hair

That came undone

When I was twenty-one

But you've seen what can happen:

But now the days are short, I'm in the autumn of the year

And now I think of my life as a vintage wine

From fine old kegs

From the brim to the dregs

It poured sweet and clear

IT WAS A VERY GOOD YEAR

A Refrain usually comes either at the beginning or the end of a verse. In older "Standards" of the 30's and 40's it usually came at the beginning of the Verse. Recently it comes more often at the end. What is important is:

1. It contains the CENTRAL IDEA
2. It is *part* of the Verse
3. It is repeated in other Verses
4. It is NOT a separate section

The content of a Refrain should be the CENTRAL IDEA of the Verse. The rest of the Verse develops or leads up to this Central idea. The Refrain contains the TITLE of the song, but can contain other repeated material.

Hook

In lyrics, "HOOK" means (or should mean) "TITLE." It is the focused statement of the CENTRAL IDEA. You should put it in the most important places in your lyric: in the balancing position; in the deceptive position; in the unexpected position; first and/or last in your Chorus.

BUILDING SECTIONS

By the time you finish this chapter, you will have a better sense of how to build the most typical lyric sections. You will also be very tired of candy bars. I used the same verse again and again to show that it is structure, not content, that makes a section what it is.

In general, balance or symmetry stop motion, while imbalance or asymmetry push forward. This is balanced:

Love me like a candy bar

Sugar, try my flavor

Let me be your chocolate star

Layer after layer

Here is its description:

BALANCE:	x SYMMETRICAL	___ ASYMMETRICAL	
PACE:	x CONSTANT	___ ACCELERATED	___ DECELERATED
FLOW:	x THROUGH-WRITTEN	___ FRAGMENTED	
CLOSURE:	x CLOSED	___ OPEN	
C. TYPE:	x EXPECTED	___ UNEXPECTED	___ DECEPTIVE

This structure would work well as either a Verse or a Chorus, though as a verse it could also be a little more unbalanced. Time to get practical. Remember these?

1. Number of phrases
2. Length of phrases
3. Rhythm of phrases
4. Rhyme scheme

We will use each one to juggle the candy bar verse. Our goal is to make different kinds of lyric sections.

First, *number of phrases*. We can unbalance the structure by *adding* a phrase without a rhyme:

> #1A.   Love me like a candy bar
>
> Sugar, try my flavor
>
> Let me be your chocolate star
>
> Smooth and rich and sweet
>
> Layer after layer

BALANCE: ___ SYMMETRICAL   _x_ ASYMMETRICAL
PACE: ___ CONSTANT   ___ ACCELERATED   _x_ DECELERATED
FLOW: _x_ THROUGH-WRITTEN   ___ FRAGMENTED
CLOSURE: _x_ CLOSED   ___ OPEN
C. TYPE: _x_ EXPECTED   ___ UNEXPECTED   ___ DECEPTIVE

Now use added phrases that rhyme:

> #1B   Love me like a candy bar
>
> Sugar, try my flavor
>
> Let me be your chocolate crunch
>
> Let me be your honey brunch
>
> Layer after layer

BALANCE: ___ SYMMETRICAL   _x_ ASYMMETRICAL
PACE: ___ CONSTANT   _x_ ACCELERATED   ___ DECELERATED
FLOW: ___ THROUGH-WRITTEN   _x_ FRAGMENTED
CLOSURE: _x_ CLOSED   ___ OPEN
C. TYPE: ___ EXPECTED   _x_ UNEXPECTED   ___ DECEPTIVE

Next, *length of phrases:*

> #2.   Love me like a candy bar
>
> Sugar, try my flavors
>
> Let me be your chocolate star
>
> Layer after *milky layer*

BALANCE: ___ SYMMETRICAL   _x_ ASYMMETRICAL
PACE: _x_ CONSTANT   ___ ACCELERATED   ___ DECELERATED
FLOW: _x_ THROUGH-WRITTEN   ___ FRAGMENTED
CLOSURE: _x_ CLOSED   ___ OPEN
C. TYPE: ___ EXPECTED   ___ UNEXPECTED   _x_ DECEPTIVE

Now, *rhythm of phrases:*

#3.   Love me like a candy bar

Layer after layer

Let me be your chocolate star

Sugar I'm bursting with flavor

(The phrase length here doesn't change, practically speaking, since the number of stressed syllables is the same.)

Finally, *rhyme scheme:*

#4.   Love me like a candy bar

Sugar, try my flavors

Let me be your chocolate star

Your Milky Way and *Mars*

BALANCE: __ SYMMETRICAL   _x_ ASYMMETRICAL

PACE: __ CONSTANT   _x_ ACCELERATED   __ DECELERATED

FLOW: _x_ THROUGH-WRITTEN   __ FRAGMENTED

CLOSURE: _x_ CLOSED   __ OPEN

C. TYPE: __ EXPECTED   __ UNEXPECTED   _x_ DECEPTIVE

Each of these altered sections keeps its identity as an independent section, but the unbalancing also leaves them hanging a little. It creates a tension that could be resolved by reaching a more balanced section.

1. *Number of phrases*

#1A might be a Verse. It closes the way you expect it to, but the added phrase puts space between rhymes, slowing the section down. It delays closure like Verse 2 of "CAN'T FIGHT THIS FEELING," so 1A might also a be good verse 2.

#1A	Melt me down like butterscotch	VERSE
	Sweet as golden honey	
	Cherries dipped in creamy fudge	
	Chocolate Easter Bunny	
	Love me like a candy bar	VERSE
	Sugar, try my flavor	
	Let me be your chocolate star	
	Smooth and rich and sweet	
	Layer after layer	
	OH HENRY, I'll be Forever Yours,	CHORUS
	'Till Mars deserts the Milky Way	
	and kids desert the candy stores	
	OH HENRY, I've lost my self control	
	Get ready for a Marathon	
	Make your Tootsie Roll	

Could #1A be a Bridge? Maybe, but be careful. A Bridge should sound completely different *right from its very first phrase.* If you used #1A as a Bridge after the Verse/Chorus Song System above, it would sound like a verse for the first three phrases. There would be no contrast, no "release" until too late.

Song System   Melt me down like butterscotch   VERSE
                 Sweet as golden honey
                 Cherries dipped in creamy fudge
                 Chocolate Easter Bunny

                     OH HENRY, I'll be Forever Yours,   CHORUS
                     Till Mars deserts the Milky Way
                     and kids desert the candy stores
                     OH HENRY, I've lost my self control
                     Get ready for a Marathon
                     Make your Tootsie Roll

                         Love me like a candy bar
                         Sugar, try my flavor
                         Let me be your chocolate star
                         Smooth and rich and sweet
                         Layer after layer

EXERCISE 29: REWRITE THE "CANDY BAR" SECTION ABOVE AS A BRIDGE SO IT WILL CONTRAST WITH THE SONG SYSTEM IT FOLLOWS. YOU MIGHT START BY SHORTENING THE FIRST PHRASE TO MAKE IT SOUND DIFFERENT RIGHT AWAY.

Rewrite:

NOW, REWRITE THE *VERSE* INSTEAD TO MAKE #1A WORK AS A BRIDGE AS IT STANDS.

Rewrite of "Melt me down. . .:"

Let's try the next one.

#1B   Love me like a candy bar

Sugar, try my flavor

Let me be your chocolate crunch

Let me be your honey brunch

Layer after layer

#1B is accelerated by its rhymes, but not its phrase lengths. Its rhythm closes DECEPTIVELY after the fourth phrase; the rhyme scheme closes UNEXPECTEDLY. Spotlights blaze on.

The section *fragments* between phrases four and five, making the last phrase UNEXPECTED. It will probably force the music of the section into an abnormal number of bars, probably either 5 or 10.

If the accelerating phrases were shorter it would fit into 4 or 8 bars smoothly:

Love me like a candy bar

Sugar, try my flavor

A chocolate crunch

A honey brunch

Layer after layer

With its longer third and fourth phrases, it is probably too unbalanced for a Chorus, though stranger things have happened.

I like it best as a Verse, especially in an A A B A form. It might work as a Bridge, as long as the other sections were different enough.

2. *Length of phrases*

The lengthening of the last phrase in #2

Love me like a candy bar

Sugar, try my flavors

Let me be your chocolate star

Layer after *milky layer*

creates a Deceptive Closure, unbalancing the section and turning spotlights on its last phrase, especially the *third stress* where the section should have closed, and the *last stress* where it actually does close.

#2 could serve as a Bridge, as long as it works as a contrast to the other sections in its lyric.

It could easily work as a Verse, perhaps best as a slightly unbalanced second verse. In either case, whether you use it as a Bridge or a Verse, be careful. What you turn spotlights on should be worthy of attention. Be sure to put important ideas in spotlighted positions.

Finally, #2 could be used as a Chorus. Here the spotlighting is important. It should spotlight the CENTRAL IDEA, perhaps like this:

LOVE ME LIKE A CANDY BAR

Sugar, try my flavors

Let me be your chocolate star

LOVE ME LIKE A CANDY BAR

As you can see, repeating the first phrase gives you a rhythmic Deception *plus* a rhyme Deception for very strong spotlighting.

EXERCISE 30: WRITE A VERSE TO LEAD UP TO THE CHORUS VERSION OF #2 JUST ABOVE. MAKE IT CONTRAST IN PHRASE LENGTH AND RHYME SCHEME.

    VERSE:

    CHORUS: LOVE ME LIKE A CANDY BAR
                 Sugar, try my flavor
                 Let me be your chocolate star
                 LOVE ME LIKE A CANDY BAR

3. *Rhythm of phrases*

Rhythm accelerates in the last phrase of #3:

        Love me like a candy bar
        Layer after layer
        Let me be your chocolate star
        Sugar I'm bursting with flavor

This has two effects:

1. Though it closes, it pushes forward. So you could use it as a last move before you get to a CENTRAL SECTION.
2. By moving to triple meter, the last phrase withholds the expected three-stress duple resolution.

    (´ ˘ ´ ˘ ´)

This makes the duple figure available to you later as a resolving figure, say as a Title opening its following section:

Love me like a candy bar	VERSE
Layer after layer	
Let me be your chocolate star	
Sugar I'm bursting with flavor	(withholding)
YOURS, FOREVER YOURS	(delivering)
You won't need any more	CHORUS
With all I've got in store	
I'M YOURS, FOREVER YOURS	

Watch how this triplet trick is used in "CAN'T FIGHT THIS FEELING" at the end of the TRANSITIONAL BRIDGE.

Verse 2 sets up a 5-stress duple phrase, then shortens the phrases at the end of the Verse to avoid closing on a five-stress phrase:

I tell myself that I can't hold out forever   VERSE 2
I say there is no reason for my fear
'Cause I feel so secure when we're together
You give my life direction   (withholding)
You make everything so clear   (withholding)

Phrase Length and Number of Phrases conspire to unbalance the section. It is closed because of the rhyme, but without the benefit of the five-stress phrase you expected.

Then, the final tease. The three-stress phrases of the Transitional Bridge finally give way to a five-stress phrase, this time in triples:

And even as I wander   TRANS
I'm keeping you in sight   BRIDGE
You're a candle in my window
On a cold dark winter's night
And I'm getting closer than I ever thought that I might

(All the grey areas in the last phrase give the music a chance to yank it into even triples. I scanned it deferring to the musical yanking.)

The delay is maddening. The long last phrase accelerates its rhythm but slows down because of its length. It still refuses to state the resolving 5-stress duple phrase. Then, at last, Ta Da, the Chorus and the Title:

I can't fight this feeling any more. . .   CHORUS

Two neat delaying tactics set up the Title. Nice juggling. You could use

Sugar I'm bursting with flavor

the same way, though not as the end of a Transitional Bridge. It is too balanced for a Transitional Bridge, and it pushes forward too hard at the wrong place to be a Chorus. It might be a Bridge. I would use the section as a Verse.

EXERCISE 31: WRITE TWO OTHER VERSIONS OF THE "CANDY BAR" SECTION, JUGGLING PHRASE RHYTHMS. MAKE SURE THAT BOTH CLOSE. WHAT EFFECTS DO YOUR VERSIONS HAVE? WHAT COULD THEY BE USED FOR?

Version 1.

EFFECT:

USES:

Version 2.

EFFECT:

USES:

4. *Rhyme scheme*

> Love me like a candy bar
>
> Sugar, try my flavors
>
> Let me be your chocolate star
>
> Your Milky Way and *Mars*

The rhyme Deception spotlights the last stress of the last phrase. Make sure you put something important there.

The section is pretty well balanced. It would be useful as a verse, perhaps as a second verse in a Verse/Verse/Chorus Song System. It might be a good Chorus Structure, but again, I'd like to see the spotlighted last phrase used as a title spot:

> Sugar I'm your CANDY BAR
>
> Come on, try my flavors
>
> Love me like a chocolate star
>
> I'm your CANDY BAR

But the closing phrase loses some punch, since its 3-stress phrase rhymes with a four-stress phrase. I'd extend the phrase too. Our earlier try at a Chorus was better:

> LOVE ME LIKE A CANDY BAR
>
> Sugar, try my flavors
>
> Let me be your chocolate star
>
> LOVE ME LIKE A CANDY BAR

Juggle juggle.

EXERCISE 32: WRITE TWO OTHER VERSIONS OF THE "CANDY BAR" SECTION, JUGGLING YOUR RHYME SCHEMES. MAKE SURE THAT BOTH CLOSE. WHAT EFFECTS DO YOUR VERSIONS HAVE? WHAT COULD THEY BE USED FOR?

Version 1.

EFFECT:

USES:

Version 2.

EFFECT:

USES:

Writing a Transitional Bridge takes more radical moves. One could look more like this:

> Love me like a candy bar
>
> Milky Way and Mars

This is unbalanced. It pushes forward, though it still feels like a section. Even a Transitional Bridge should feel like a section. Here *rhyme* takes care of the feeling of section, while the shorter phrase length kicks the supports out from under the section.

EXERCISE 33: WRITE TWO MORE TRANSITIONAL BRIDGES, USING THE "CANDY BAR" SECTION. JUGGLE WHATEVER YOU LIKE, BUT MAKE SURE THAT BOTH CAN BE IDENTIFIED AS SECTIONS. WHAT EFFECTS DO YOUR VERSIONS HAVE?

Version 1.

EFFECT:

Version 2.

EFFECT:

You have looked at typical elements or sections of lyrics. It is important to put them together carefully so they can do their jobs, arranging phrases to make sections move or stop appropriately. Learn the niceties of juggling *number of phrases, phrase lengths, rhythms, and rhymes*. It helps, especially when you write whole lyrics. The same techniques time after time get less and less effective. Always be on the lookout for new ways to turn on the lights.

CHAPTER SIX
Song Forms: the Big Show

In the same way you juggle the phrases of sections, you can learn to juggle sections to make Song Systems, or to make full lyrics. The same principles apply on each level.

Verse/Refrain

Look at the principle behind the limerick:

> There once was a student named Esser
>
> Whose knowledge grew lesser and lesser
>
> It at last grew so small, he knew nothing at all
>
> And now he's a college professor

The principle is simple:

1.	STATEMENT OF STRUCTURE	A
2.	RESTATEMENT OF STRUCTURE	A
3.	VARIATION OF STRUCTURE	B
4.	RETURN TO ORIGINAL STRUCTURE	A

Repeating the structure of the first statement defines "home base." Moving away from home base at the third phrase creates tension — a move to unfamiliar territory. Coming back to familiar territory at phrase four is a resolution, a welcome home party.

The principle works the same way for *lyric sections* as it does for phrases. It can work as a principle for building *entire lyrics*.

Let's use the principle on a lyric that has only verses. Then we will add a Bridge. Here are the Verses:

THIS BOTTLE AND ME

	We've been sitting here the whole night long
	Pouring out our hearts
	About how loving never ends the way
V. 1	We felt it at the start
	And we'll sit right here till we decide
	What the next step ought to be
	We got a lot to talk about
	THIS BOTTLE AND ME

	We started off all full of hope
	That things would work out fine
	But drinking from the loving cup
V. 2	We somehow missed the signs
	Sip by sip we used it up
	Now it's empty as can be
	We got a lot to talk about
	THIS BOTTLE AND ME

When the sun has set and I need a friend

And there's no one else around

I open up the cupboard

V. 3   Take this empty bottle down

It's the last one I was drinking

When my drinking made her leave

We got a lot to talk about

THIS BOTTLE AND ME

This lyric has a REFRAIN:

We got a lot to talk about

THIS BOTTLE AND ME

Part of the Refrain is the HOOK,

THIS BOTTLE AND ME

The Refrain is a part of the verse's phrase and rhyme structure.

	We've been sitting here the whole night long	x
A	Pouring out our hearts	a
	About how loving never ends the way	x
	We felt it at the start	a
	And we'll sit right here 'till we decide	x
A	What the next step ought to be	b
	We got a lot to talk about	x
	THIS BOTTLE AND ME	b

The rhythm of each verse goes twice through the basic Common Meter structure. Each verse rhymes x a x a x b x b.

The structure and the content of each verse fragment the section after line 4, making each of the three verses subdivide into two parts (1) A A, (2) A A, (3) A A. The Refrain in this lyric appears at the end of each verse.

Because of all the repetition of structure, this lyric gets boring fast. It needs a release from all the repetition. You could consider a Bridge in this situation. It would accomplish three things:

1. It would break up the monotony of the same pattern. This will also set up the last verse with a contrasting section.

2. It would give different size Song Systems:

    S1 { A

    S2 { A

          B

    S3 {

          A

This breaks the repetition of the same size pattern. With only verses, each Song System is the *length of each verse.* Adding a Bridge creates another Song System that starts at the Bridge and ends when the last verse closes.

3.   A Bridge would also give the verse ideas a chance to "breathe" by moving to a new angle or perspective.

Here it is with a Bridge:

THIS BOTTLE AND ME

V. 1
> We've been sitting here the whole night long
>
> Pouring out our hearts
>
> About how loving never ends the way
>
> We felt it at the start
>
> And we'll sit right here till we decide
>
> What the next step ought to be
>
> We got a lot to talk about
>
> THIS BOTTLE AND ME

V. 2
> We started off all full of hope
>
> That things would work out fine
>
> But drinking from the loving cup
>
> We somehow missed the signs
>
> Sip by sip we used it up
>
> Now it's empty as can be
>
> We got a lot to talk about
>
> THIS BOTTLE AND ME

Bridge
> THIS BOTTLE AND ME will do all right
>
> We'll just stay right here together
>
> Waste away the night
>
> Waiting till the morning comes
>
> And the ache is almost gone
>
> Struggle through another day
>
> Till another night comes rolling on

The Bridge is asymmetrical, containing 7 phrases. It is different from the verses in both rhythm and rhyme:

This bottle and me will do all *right*	a
We'll just stay right here together	x
Waste away the *night*	a
Waiting 'till the morning comes	x
And the ache is almost *gone*	b
Struggle through another day	x
'Till another night comes rolling *on*	b

Though the rhythm of the Bridge is based on Common Meter (especially in the last four lines), it is different where a difference *needs* to be made —in its *first line* where it is clearly a rhythmic departure; and in its *last line* where the extra stressed syllable is a rhythmic Deception. It moves forward to form the new Song System:

Bridge
> THIS BOTTLE AND ME will do all right
>
> We'll just stay right here together
>
> Waste away the night
>
> Waiting till the morning comes
>
> And the ache is almost gone
>
> Struggle through another day
>
> Till another night comes rolling on

V. 3
> When the sun has set and I need a friend
>
> And there's no one else around
>
> I open up the cupboard
>
> Take this empty bottle down
>
> It's the last one I was drinking
>
> When my drinking made her leave
>
> We got a lot to talk about
>
> THIS BOTTLE AND ME

The move into the last verse returns to home base, resolving the tension created by moving away.

VERSE/CHORUS

If the A A B A song form works on the principle of the limerick, the simple Verse/Chorus form works on the principle of Common Meter (also called the "Ballad Stanza").

> O Western Wind, when will thou blow
>
> That the small rain down can rain?
>
> Christ, that my love were in my arms
>
> And I in my bed again
>
> — Anonymous

Or this:

> The wind doth blow today my love
>
> And a few small drops of rain
>
> I never had but one true love
>
> In cold grave she was lain
>
> — From "The Unquiet Grave," Anonymous

Again, the principle is simple

1.	STATEMENT	A
2.	NEW STATEMENT	B
3.	RESTATEMENT OF #1'S STRUCTURE	A
4.	RESTATEMENT OF #2'S STRUCTURE	B

Now look at a lyric that chains its elements together in the same way:

SOUTHERN COMFORT

Spanish moss hanging low   VERSE
Swaying from the trees
Honeysuckle, sweet magnolia
Riding on the breeze
Southern evenings, southern stars
Used to bring me peace
But now they only make me cry
They only make me realize

    There's no SOUTHERN COMFORT   CHORUS
    Unless you're in my arms
    You're the only cure
    For this aching in my heart
    I've searched everywhere
    Tried the bedrooms, tried the bars
    But there's no SOUTHERN COMFORT
    Unless you're in my arms

Ruby-throated Whipporwills   VERSE
Gliding down the sky
Evenings lonely on the porch
You slip back on my mind
SOUTHERN COMFORT after dark
Helps me face the night
But there's nothing to look forward to
'Cept looking back to loving you

    There's no SOUTHERN COMFORT   CHORUS
    Unless you're in my arms
    You're the only cure
    For this aching in my heart
    I've searched everywhere
    Tried the bedrooms, tried the bars
    But there's no SOUTHERN COMFORT
    Unless you're in my arms

The rhythm of verse one is basically Common Meter for the first six phrases:

Spanish moss hanging low   x
Swaying from the trees   a
Honeysuckle, sweet magnolia   x
Riding on the breeze   a
Southern evenings, southern stars   x
Used to bring me peace   a

By the time we get through the first six phrases we are locked into Common meter. The seventh phrase only continues the pattern:

But now they only make me cry   b

Surely everybody on the planet will expect a three-stress Common Meter close. Now that you have their attention, it is time for a little surprise:

They only make me realize   b

Both the rhythm and the rhyme structure unbalance the Verse with a Deceptive Closure:

low	x
trees	a
magnolia	x
breeze	a
stars	x
peace	a
cry	b
realize	b

The DECEPTIVE closure unbalances the Verse. It spotlights the last phrase and calls special attention to the forward direction of the Song System: "Makes me realize . . . what?" The Verse has done its job: it has created a clear section, and has also pointed to where it wants to go.

The last phrase of this verse, *and the last phrase alone,* unbalances the section. It leaves you high and dry with your expectations for a three-stress closure unrequited. It is nice that the Verse leaves you wanting something, especially when the Chorus delivers it in spades.

There's no Southern Comfort
Unless you're in my arms
You're the only cure
For this aching in my heart
I've searched everywhere
Tried the bedrooms, tried the bars
But there's no Southern Comfort
Unless you're in my arms

With the exception of line 6, every line has three stresses. Line 6 has 2 phrases, accelerating at that point. The final two phrases return to three stresses. Any three-stress phrase *would have balanced the verse!* But the verse has refused to deliver. Not until you reach the Chorus ("home base") do you hear what you wanted to.

The rhythm is not regular in the HOOK:

There's no Southern Comfort

So you have to wait for a repetition of the HOOK to balance the section rhythmically.

The rhyme structure of the Chorus also gives us what we wanted in the verse but didn't get:

comfort	x
arms	a
cure	x
heart	a
where	x
bars	a
comfort	x
arms	a

Both the rhyme and the rhythm deliver what the Verse set up: balance in rhyme and a three-stress last phrase. The Song System Closes. Motion is stopped.

Verse

{

Chorus

EXERCISE 34: SCAN THE SECOND VERSE FOR RHYTHM AND LOOK AT ITS RHYME STRUCTURE TO SEE IF IT IS PARALLEL TO THE FIRST VERSE. DO VERSE 2 AND THE SECOND CHORUS FORM A SECOND SONG SYSTEM?

Ruby-throated Whippoorwills

Gliding down the sky

Evenings lonely on the porch

You slip back on my mind

SOUTHERN COMFORT after dark

Helps me face the night

But there's nothing to look forward to

'cept looking back to loving you

Rhyme structure:_____

Comments:

You have been through two Song Systems. The lyric ends here nicely. A B A B delivers a very effective punch.

If you wanted to add more to the A B A B system above, you should probably think about a Bridge instead of another verse. As you saw in the A A B A song form, too much repetition gets boring fast. A Bridge would accomplish three things:

1. It would break up the monotony of the same pattern. This will also move into the last chorus from a new angle, a contrasting section.

2. Assuming that the Bridge is shorter than the Verses (most of the time it is), it would give you different sizes of Song Systems:

$$
S1 \left\{ \begin{array}{l} V \\[2ex] CH \end{array} \right.
$$

$$
S2 \left\{ \begin{array}{l} V \\[2ex] CH \end{array} \right.
$$

$$
S3 \left\{ \begin{array}{l} B \\[2ex] CH \end{array} \right.
$$

This breaks the repetition of the same pattern. S1 and S2 are the same size. S3 will be shorter, giving the Chorus a boost in interest when you get to it "early."

3. A Bridge would also give the idea a chance to "breathe" by releasing to a new angle or perspective.

How do you approach putting together a Bridge structure? Do you just start writing and see what happens? Probably not, since you need to write a contrasting section. You at least need to know *not to write* what you already have. So you look at what you have.

In SOUTHERN COMFORT the phrases are both 3-stress and 4-stress phrases, PLUS quick passes at 2-stress phrases in:

Southern evenings, southern stars

and in

Tried the bedrooms, tried the bars

Where 2-stress phrases have appeared, they have been in non-resolving places. I like the idea of taking the hint and developing it for the Bridge, at least to start. Here is my result:

Bar to bar
Face to face
Someone else takes your place
But no one's ever new
I always turn them into you

Start with fast 2-stress phrases (as you dive into the singles bar lifestyle) for contrast and a push forward. Now build the section into longer phrases, slowing it down until you realize (with a sigh at the futility of it all),

But no one's ever new

I always turn them into you

The final realization comes in the restated Chorus:

There's no SOUTHERN COMFORT	CHORUS
Unless you're in my arms	
You're the only cure	
For this aching in my heart	
I've searched everywhere	
Tried the bedrooms, tried the bars	
But there's no SOUTHERN COMFORT	
Unless you're in my arms	

EXERCISE 35: WRITE A BRIDGE OF YOUR OWN FOR "SOUTHERN COMFORT."

Now look at a lyric with a Transitional Bridge.

TEDDY DOESN'T LIVE HERE ANYMORE

Song System 1:

Teddy feels alone again	VERSE 1
It happens every night	
There inside his room again	
He listens as they fight	
Tonight it will be different	VERSE 2
Leaving while they sleep	
He sneaks into the closed garage	
Tonight he'll find peace	
Crying "Mama won't you listen!	TRANS BR 1
Daddy can't you see!"	
He slides the seat back	
Turns the key	

It's a short ride to the dark side   CHORUS
All the love he might have known
Lost forever, left alone
No one in the world could hear
The closing of the door
TEDDY DOESN'T LIVE HERE ANYMORE

Song System 2:

Years go by like passing clouds   VERSE 3
People soon forget
But at a party in a crowd
The girl he should have met

She feels a longing, feels a pull
From somewhere she can't see
While Teddy from the other side
Struggles to break free

He cries, "Baby, it's so cold here   TRANS BR 2
Won't you take me home?"
She shivers as she turns away
Leaves alone

It's a short ride to the dark side   CHORUS
All the love he might have known
Lost forever, left alone
No one in the world could hear
The closing of the door
TEDDY DOESN'T LIVE HERE ANYMORE

Song System 3:

Just sixteen   BRIDGE
He couldn't see
Where life ahead of him might lead
He couldn't see at sweet sixteen
What could have been

It's a short ride to the dark side   CHORUS
All the love he might have known
Lost forever, left alone
No one in the world could hear
The closing of the door
TEDDY DOESN'T LIVE HERE ANYMORE
TEDDY DOESN'T LIVE HERE ANYMORE

A clear Common Meter opening, setting the pattern.

> Teddy feels alone again   x
> It happens every night   a
> There inside his room again   x
> He listens as they fight   a

By now you are ready for some "Second Verse Strategy:"

> Tonight it will be diff'rent
> Leaving while they sleep
> He sneaks into the closed garage
> Tonight he'll find peace

This verse is slightly unbalanced because of the last phrase. Two stressed syllables in a row force an irregular rhythm. Yet it would have been easy to write a regular rhythm:

> Tonight he'll find his peace

The irregular rhythm creates tension at a place of strong tension in the ideas. Besides the Prosody, the unbalancing moves the section on, even though you know you are at the end of a section. The imperfect rhyme of "sleep/peace" defines the section too, but still lets you feel the pull forward. So verse 2 tips forward into the Transitional Bridge:

> Crying "Mama won't you listen!   x
> Daddy can't you see!"   a
> He slides the seat back   x
> Turns the key   a

The opening phrase of the Transitional Bridge is the longest phrase so far in the lyric. The lyric slows down like it was walking through molasses. (Interesting, though: if the composer of the music chooses to, the song can actually accelerate here by squeezing this long phrase into a short space. The overall result of the squeeze could be a frantic feeling that matches Teddy's.)

This long phrase has another important effect: because it ends on an unstressed syllable, it implies a 5th stressed syllable.

> Crying "Mama won't you listen (now)!

Without knowing it, your listener is being set up for the only 5-stress phrase in the song: the HOOK! The second phrase is shorter, and, with the four stresses of the first line, hints at Common Meter:

> Daddy can't you see!"

The third phrase is even shorter, and, like the third phrase of verse 2, irregular:

> He slides the seat back

Finally, the coup de grace:

> Turns the key

You can feel the tension as the lines get shorter and Teddy's life closes, too abruptly, too early.

EXERCISE 36: REWRITE THE TRANSITIONAL BRIDGE SO THAT IT MOVES FROM SHORTER PHRASES TO LONGER ONES. TRY TO MOVE IT EVEN FURTHER FROM THE VERSE STRUCTURE BY CHANGING THE RHYME SCHEME. WHAT EFFECT DO YOU THINK THE X A X A RHYME SCHEME HAS? HOW WOULD YOU HAVE DONE IT?

The Chorus lands on a rhythm figure that has been carefully set up in Verse Two and the Transitional Bridge:

> It's a short ride to the dark side

It feels like "home," but is too unbalanced to let you rest. The internal rhyme accelerates and pushes you ahead into

> all the love he might have known

a balanced 4-stress phrase that moves forward to seek a rhyme:

> Lost forever, left alone

Even with the rhyme, the section is still unbalanced here because of the odd number of phrases. Keep going.

> No one in the world could hear
> the closing of the door

This is the longest phrase in the Song System. Now we are ready for the release into the 5-stress Hook and a rhyme closure.

> Teddy doesn't live here anymore

The most important and spotlighted phrase in the Song system.

EXERCISE 37: TRY SETTING UP THE HOOK BY USING SHORTER PHRASES INSTEAD OF THE LONG PHRASE:

> No one in the world could hear
> the closing of the door

Try to create a sense of arrival with your shorter phrases;
make a couple of tries:

1. (maybe try / ⌣ / ⌣ / ⌣ , / ⌣ / ⌣ /)

TEDDY DOESN'T LIVE HERE ANYMORE

2.

TEDDY DOESN'T LIVE HERE ANYMORE

I think of the longer phrase as the rubber of a slingshot, stretching to give power to the release. It seems to me that it should be longer than the Hook, especially since there are no 5-stress lines to set up expectations for a 5-stress close.

After the two new verses, the second Transitional Bridge changes its content, but keeps in close parallel with the first.

> He cries, "Baby, it's so cold here
>
> Won't you take me home?"
>
> She shivers as she turns away
>
> Leaves alone

The third line retains the same number of strong stresses as

> He slídes the seát báck

The additional unstressed syllables shiver quickly past and leave with her. The change forces the music to accelerate by stuffing syllables between the strong positions. In this case, the effect could be startling. Normally, though, keep your sections parallel.

Finally, the Bridge:

> Just sixteen
>
> He couldn't see
>
> Where life ahead of him might lead
>
> He couldn't see at sweet sixteen
>
> What could have been

This section seems very unbalanced: three balanced 4-stress rhythms end *two stresses short* in the last line, with just a whiff of rhyme in "see/lead/teen/been." Scan it.

> Júst síxteén. Hé couldn't sée
>
> Whére life ahéad óf hím might léad
>
> Hé couldn't sée at sweét síxteén
>
> What could have beén

The first phrases play off against the rhythms, grouping this way:

> Just sixteen
>
> He couldn't see where life ahead of him might lead

The Bridge starts fast, then slows with the long second phrase. The last phrase sort of floats away. Like Teddy's chances for love.

Sometimes a Transitional Bridge leads, NOT to a separate Chorus, but to a Refrain.

YOU NEVER LET ME DOWN

Song system 1:	Turned loose in a company of strangers	VERSE 1
	Getting nowhere, we had nowhere to go	
	Bad blues hit you harder when you're aching	
	They never leave you, they'll never leave you alone	
	They get you crawlin'	
	I might've fallen	TRANS BR 1
	But you were always around	
	YOU NEVER LET ME DOWN	REFRAIN
	YOU NEVER LET ME DOWN	
Song system 2:	Tough kids growing up like we were brothers	VERSE 2
	Making trouble, barely making it through	
	Quick hitch, Viet Nam was tougher	
	I didn't worry, I was counting on you	
	Fightin' dirty	TRANS BR 2
	Might'a hurt me	
	But you were always around	
	YOU NEVER LET ME DOWN	REFRAIN
	YOU NEVER LET ME DOWN	
Song system 3:	You were so much more than a friend	
	Again and again	
	Those years flood back	BRIDGE
	As I trace your name	
	With those engraved	
	On marble black, black and smooth	
	Some things will never change	
	I still lean on you	
	No tears for times we shared together	VERSE 3
	Know you'd want it, I know you'd want it that way	
	Slow years ticking by as I remember	
	Touching you now makes them easy to face	
	It's like you're still here	TRANS BR 3
	I feel you so clear	
	It's like you're always around	
	YOU NEVER LET ME DOWN	REFRAIN
	YOU NEVER LET ME DOWN	

The difference between the Verse section and the next section is clear. The Verse moves in longer phrases, using imperfect rhymes separated by distance.

Turned loose in a company of strangers   a
Getting nowhere, we had nowhere to go   b
Bad blues hit you harder when you're aching   a
They won't leave you, they won't leave you alone   b

Now, the contrasting section. Short phrases. Quick rhymes.

They get you crawlin'
I might've fallen

and the set-up: 3-stress line and a sound for the HOOK to attach to:

But you were always around

Leading to the Refrain:

YOU NEVER LET ME DOWN

And the Song System closes down on the title.

EXERCISE 38: CHANGE THE TRANSITIONAL BRIDGE OF "YOU NEVER LET ME DOWN" SO IT FORMS AN UNBALANCED SECTION BY ITSELF. THEN DEVELOP THE CHORUS INTO A SEPARATE SYSTEM.

Trans Br:

Chorus:

CHAPTER SEVEN
HOOK PLACEMENT AND FOCUS: TURNING THE LIGHTS ON

Your HOOK is the hero of your lyric. It belongs in the spotlight, the most important place in your lyric. But putting it there is up to you. *You* have to put it in focus. You can't just toss your HOOK anywhere and hope the light shines on it — you have to choose where and when to turn the spotlight on. You must *refuse to let the light shine anyplace else.* Here are five useful strategies for putting your HOOK in lights.

1. Put the HOOK at the beginning or end of its section, maybe both.
2. Keep your structure moving forward until you get to the HOOK.
3. Repeat the HOOK.
4. Use sound to spotlight your HOOK.
5. Use the HOOK's rhythm in other strategic places.

Let's take a quick tour.

1. *Put the HOOK at the beginning or end of its section, maybe both.*

This one is easy, but it is worth looking at. What it really says is that lights are brighter at the beginnings and ends of sections than in the spaces between. Here is a Chorus where the HOOK comes first.

> EIGHTEEN WHEELS AND A DOZEN ROSES
>
> Ten more miles on his four lane run
>
> A few more songs from the all night radio
>
> And he'll spend the rest of his life
>
> with the one that he loves
>
>   — Paul and Gene Nelson

Note that the *last* phrase in the chorus is also an important idea. Here is a Steely Dan Chorus with the HOOK at the end:

> O, No Hesitation
>
> No tears and no hearts breaking
>
> No remorse
>
> O, Congratulations!
>
> This is your HAITIAN DIVORCE
>
>   — Donald Fagen, Walter Becker, "HAITIAN DIVORCE"

Now a Jim Rushing Chorus with the HOOK at both places:

> A SLOW HEALING HEART
>
> Is dying to mend
>
> Longing for love
>
> Lonely again
>
> When a spirit is broken
>
> And the memories start
>
> Nothing moves slower
>
> Than A SLOW HEALING HEART

You have the same strategies available when your *Verse* contains the HOOK, though most of the time when you write a Verse/Refrain, you will use your HOOK *either* at the beginning *or* at the end, usually not both. If you use it both places, you will have to use it twice in every verse. In most cases, that would be too much.

Beginnings and endings. Two HOT SPOTS.

EXERCISE 39: Write a balanced Chorus using the following title at the beginning. Then, rewrite it with the same title at the end.

YOU DON'T HAVE THE BEST OF ME YET

Title First:

Title Last:

Even in sections where you don't have a HOOK, you must still pay attention to beginnings and endings. The beginning and end of any *section* should be as interesting as you can make them.

Look at these beginnings and endings:

> First: They'll buy a Winnebago . . .
> Last: Leavin' every other reason behind
> — Gene and Paul Nelson

> First: Your mother will try to protect you . . .
> Last: That's something that I understand
> — John Jarvis, Gary Nicholson

> First: Across the street the Randall's oldest daughter
> must have come home . . .
> Last: And I thought of what I'd give to feel another
> summer linger when a day feels like a year
> — Beth Nielsen Chapman

EXERCISE 40: WRITE A VERSE TO SET UP YOUR CHORUS YOU WROTE FOR THE LAST EXERCISE. MAKE SURE YOU USE THE BEGINNING AND END POSITIONS FOR IMPORTANT IDEAS.

This is important: when you use beginnings and endings for their value as HOT SPOTS, you can think of it this way:

> Find your *most important ideas* and put them in the HOT SPOTS.

Or, you can think of it this way:

> *Whatever* ideas you put in HOT SPOTS *become* your most important ideas. You *make* them important by putting them there.

Imagine you have a blinking red LED in your brain set to go off every time you put something at the beginning or end of a section. That will warn you to use the positions well.

The principle of beginnings and endings applies other places.

For the lyric as a whole, it says that the opening *section* and the closing *section* must be very strong.

For the lyric as a whole, it says that the opening *phrase* and the closing *phrase* must be very strong.

For each phrase of your lyric. Prose writers use the principle of beginnings and endings as a strategy when they write sentences. They insist that the sentence's first "idea" word (noun, adjective, or verb) should be one of the most important words in the sentence. The same for the end of the sentence. Some writers go so far as to insist that, wherever possible, *the second most important word* in the sentence come at the beginning, and the *most important word* come at the *end.* There is a big difference between the following two sentences. The first puts all its substance at the end.

Compare:

1. When it happens naturally, and no one is wiser, wild sex yanks my chain.
2. Wild sex, when it happens naturally, and no one is wiser, yanks my chain.

Two "dead" clauses tread water in the first version, waiting for something to happen. The same clauses gather steam in the second version. Starting strong will color what comes afterwards.

You can apply prose writer's logic to lyric phrases. If you put something important at the *beginning* of your phrase and something important at the *end,* your phrase will show off your best ideas where they are most likely to be noticed.

Beginnings and endings. HOT SPOTS.

2. *Keep the structure pointing forward until you get to the HOOK.*

A. In CENTRAL SECTIONS, focus your structure on the HOOK:

No one else can touch you	a
I'm always gonna love you	a
It sounds old-fashioned, out of date for sure	b
Nothing could be better	c
Take this heart forever	c
Outta fashion SWEET OLD-FASHIONED GIRL	b

In this case the HOOK is at the *end* of the section. The structure pushes you forward with both rhythm and rhyme until you finally land on the HOOK. It lights up, balances, and closes.

B. In DEVELOPMENTAL SECTIONS unbalance to push forward when there is a HOOK opening the next section. (Note that your section must still feel like a section, so you can't simply leave it open.)

Too real is this feeling of make believe

Too real when I feel what my heart can't conceal

Yes I'm THE GREAT PRETENDER . . .

The rhyme throws you off balance. You expected a rhyme with "believe." Instead, "conceal" works with "real/feeling/ real/feel," to keep you off balance.

Look at this one by Jim Rushing. It is really pretty because it ends on the HOOK, but the HOOK is the shorter, unbalancing phrase, making it lean forward to arrive at — the HOOK:

There's a part of my feelings ever on guard

Against looks that are tender and words that are hard

I still remember those cutting remarks

Weak is a SLOW HEALING HEART

A SLOW HEALING HEART	CHORUS
Is dying to mend . . .	

C. Most common, simply keep your sections moving into one another:

It's a bridge you can't cross

It's a cross you can't bear

It's the words you can't say

The things you can't change

No matter how much you care

So you do all you can

Then you've gotta let go

You're just part of the flow

Of the river that runs between FATHERS AND SONS

— John Jarvis, Gary Nicholson

Scan the first part. The phrases are the same length. This is a clear case where the *number of phrases* unbalances the section and leans ahead.

Finally, Fagen and Becker at work:

> Babs and Clean Willie were in love they said
> So in love the preacher's face turned red
> Soon everybody knew the thing was dead
> He shouts,
> She bites
> They wrangle through the night
> She go crazy
> Gotta make a getaway
> Papa say
>
> O, no hesitation . . .

This one both leans and closes, almost by magic. . .

A final caution. It is not *necessary* that sections not containing a HOOK be unbalanced. There is another obvious way to move one section to the next — *musically*. If all of your lyric sections were *perfectly balanced,* the music could still move them forward. But music often appreciates and profits from a helping hand from the lyric.

3.   *Repeat the HOOK*

Your HOOK should come at least once in each Song System. That is usually enough. Within reason you can squeeze it in a few more times.

Direct repetition is simple, but effective.

> TEDDY DOESN'T LIVE HERE ANYMORE
> TEDDY DOESN'T LIVE HERE ANYMORE
>
> They get you crawlin'
> I might'a fallen
> But you were always around
> YOU NEVER LET ME DOWN
> YOU NEVER LET ME DOWN

You can make direct repetition even more effective with a special effect, like a turn in meaning:

> You were RIGHT FROM THE START
> RIGHT FROM THE START
> You had my number all along
> You were right and I was wrong
> RIGHT FROM THE START
> RIGHT FROM THE START

You can put your HOOK at both the *beginning and the end* of a section:

> Why don't you TICKLE ME
> Gee whiz won't that be fine
> What a great idea,
> What a perfect way to kill some time
> Can't stop to think
> 'Cause if we do we'll lose our minds
> Why don't you TICKLE ME
>
> — Randy Newman, "TICKLE ME"

You can end your Verse with the HOOK as a Refrain, then move to your Chorus with the HOOK in it too:

> Now when I look at my own son
>
> I know what my father went through
>
> There's only so much you can do
>
> You're proud when they walk
>
> Scared when they run
>
> That's how it always has been between FATHERS AND SONS

> It's a bridge you can't cross
>
> It's a cross you can't bear
>
> It's the words you can't say
>
> The things you can't change
>
> No matter how much you care
>
> So you do all you can
>
> Then you've gotta let go
>
> You're just part of the flow
>
> Of the river that runs
>
> Between FATHERS AND SONS

Of course, if you repeat yourself too much if you repeat yourself too much if you repeat yourself too much if you repeat yourself too much if you repeat yourself too much you get boring, so be cautious. If you can make your repetition necessary to finish the structure, all the better:

1.	My kitchen clock's on Phoenix time	a
2.	That's where you promised you'd be mine	a
3.	My watch is set for Tennessee	b
4.	The place where time ran out on me	b
5.	My bedroom's still in Boston's zone	c
6.	I wake at dawn, I rise alone,	c
7.	And though these times all disagree	b
8.	At least one thing stays true	d
9.	MY HEART'S STILL SET ON YOU	d
10.	MY HEART'S STILL SET ON YOU	d

The section is balanced by the repetition.

Or maybe like this:

> Even though you're with me
>
> Might as well be by myself
>
> 'Cause the way you look at me is like
>
> You're SEEING SOMEONE ELSE

The first two phrases are each 3-stresses at best. There are certainly some grey areas here:

> Even though you're with me
>
> Might as well be by myself

The next two lines (as written) add up to one 7-stress phrase:

'Cause the way you look at me is like
You're SEEING SOMEONE ELSE

You can hear the section close, but it still feels a little off balance. You can feel the general shape of Common Meter, plus the "self/else" rhyme, but the rhythm is a little irregular and the phrase lengths are uneven, even if you think of the first two phrases as one phrase:

Even though you're with me Might as well be by myself

It still fails to balance the last phrase. Repeating the last phrase does the trick.

> Even though you're with me
>
> Might as well be by myself
>
> 'Cause the way you look at me is like
>
> You're SEEING SOMEONE ELSE
>
> The way you look at me is like
>
> You're SEEING SOMEONE ELSE

You have made the repetition a part of the structure.

EXERCISE 41: WRITE A VERSE THAT ENDS WITH THE REFRAIN:

YOU DON'T HAVE THE BEST OF ME YET

Make a repetition necessary by using two strategies:

1. Unbalance the system by making the rhythmic closure at the Refrain awkward, like "SEEING SOMEONE ELSE."

2. Unbalance the section by making the Refrain an odd numbered phrase (5th phrase or 7th would be ideal).

4. *Use sound to spotlight the Hook.*

This technique is subtle, but very useful. I call it TARGETING. Here are two examples. Both use a vowel sound that occurs in the HOOK an *odd number of times* to prepare your ear for the HOOK. . .

For the first example, see "WHY CAN'T I HAVE YOU," (p. 62).
The second example is from Kevin Cronin:

And even as I wander	TRANS
I'm keeping you in *sight*	BRIDGE
You're a candle in my window	
On a cold dark winter's *night*	
And I'm getting closer than I ever thought that I *might*	
I CAN'T *FIGHT* THIS FEELING ANY MORE	CHORUS

This is straightforward. Three "ite" sounds set up the second most important word in the HOOK. Musically, the tonic chord comes on "feeling." Both ideas are supported and spotlighted, one by sound TARGETING in the lyric, the other by the arrival of the tonic. Neat.

EXERCISE 42: WRITE A BALANCED CHORUS THAT BEGINS AND ENDS WITH THE HOOK,

I SLIPPED AND FELL IN LOVE

Now, using "WHY CAN'T I HAVE YOU" as a model,

1. write a Transitional Bridge leading up to it that TARGETS to the vowel sound in "slipped."

2. Write a Transitional Bridge that targets to "fell."

5. *Use the HOOK's rhythm in other strategic places.*

This is a terrific strategy. It not only helps spotlight your HOOK, but it makes finding line lengths and rhythms for your verses less arbitrary. Think of this strategy in the same way composers think of melodic themes: they state their theme, then use it other places in different ways. Speed it up, slow it down, say it backwards, turn it upside down, keep its shape but change its notes, keep its notes but change its chords, keep its rhythm but change its notes and chords. They call this "Motivic Development." They use it for two reasons:

1. It is a subtle way of repeating a theme without getting boring.

2. It makes the *theme* the focus of the piece.

Though you don't need to make it nearly so complicated, you can do the same thing with the *rhythm* of your HOOK. The strategy is very simple, but it depends on you taking a very important step:

KNOW THE *RHYTHM* OF YOUR HOOK *BEFORE* YOU START WRITING YOUR LYRIC

Then use your HOOK'S rhythm in "*strategic positions.*"

I thought you'd never ask . . . A *strategic position* is a place you have to *match* in order to *balance* a section. In Common Meter, this is a strategic position:

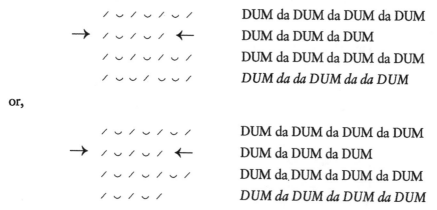

The second phrase is the strategic position — when you match it by repeating it in the fourth phrase, the section balances.

If you unbalance the system,

or,

your listener will *still* want the rhythm of the strategic position. If *the rhythm of the HOOK is in the strategic position,* your HOOK will light up when you arrive.

Applying this logic, here is a section. Line two is the strategic position:

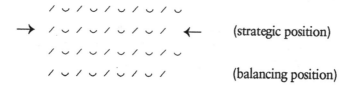

You could have prevented a match in line four by adding two shorter phrases instead of a 5-stress phrase. Like this:

```
          / ‿ / ‿ / ‿ / ‿ / ‿
→         / ‿ / ‿ / ‿ / ‿ /      ← (strategic position)
          / ‿ / ‿ / ‿ / ‿ / ‿
          { ‿ / ‿ / ‿ / ‿ }            (unbalancing phrases)
          { ‿ ‿ / ‿ / ‿ / }
```

Watch.

I tell myself I can't hold out forever
→   I say there is no reason for my fear   ← (strategic position)
'Cause I feel so secure when we're together
You give my life direction   (unbalancing phrases)
You make everything so clear

When your HOOK rhythm matches the second phrase, as in

I CAN'T FIGHT THIS FEELING ANYMORE

you will arrive in a blaze of glory.

If you look closer at Kevin Cronin's whole approach to the HOOK, you will see the HOOK rhythm used in several strategic positions.

I can't fight this feeling any longer
→   Yet I'm still afraid to let it flow

What started out as friendship has grown stronger
→   I only wish I had the strength to let it show

I tell myself that I can't hold out forever
→   I say there is no reason for my fear

'Cause I feel so secure when we're together

You give my life direction

You make everything so clear

And even as I wander

I'm keeping you in sight

You're a candle in my window

On a cold dark winter's night

And I'm getting closer than I ever thought that I might

I CAN'T FIGHT THIS FEELING ANY MORE   CHORUS

Because the first Verse actually *closes* the section with the 5-stress phrase, *not closing* with it at the end of the second verse makes it all the more tantalizing. When you hear it in triplets at the end of the Transitional Bridge, it is maddening. It is so satisfying to finally reach the 5-stress rhythm at the HOOK.

You can see how well the strategy works. Did Kevin Cronin do it on purpose? He could have. Whether or not HE did is not the point. YOU can.

Here is an interesting rhythm. Its third phrase is the strategic position.

/ ˘ / ˘ / ˘ /
/ ˘ / ˘ /
→   / ˘ / ˘ / ˘ / ˘ /
/ ˘ / ˘ / ˘ /
/ ˘ / ˘ /
/ ˘ / ˘ / ˘ /

What is interesting is that you start through it syllable by syllable, so the *second* phrase seems like the strategic position all the way until the 4th stress of the third phrase:

/ ˘ / ˘ / ˘ /
/ ˘ / ˘ /
/ ˘ / ˘ / ˘ / ...

It feels like Common Meter so far. For a second you think of

/ ˘ / ˘ /

as the resolving phrase. Although it does not turn out to be the strategic position, the fact that it *could have been* emphasizes it a little. Plus, if you *change* the fifth phrase (where you expect to hear it again) you will unbalance the system and *make* the 3-stress phrase a strategic position:

/ ˘ / ˘ / ˘ /
/ ˘ / ˘ /
→   / ˘ / ˘ / ˘ / ˘ /
→   / ˘ / ˘ / ˘
/ ˘ / ˘ / ˘
/ ˘ / ˘ / ˘ / ˘ /

Look at this Song System.

SEEING SOMEONE ELSE

I feel some changes in the air
You haven't been yourself
You been lookin' kinda dreamy off in space
Could it be the smell of perfume
That's starting up this aching
Or the secrets I see lighting up your face

When we talk you never meet my eyes
You're looking right on past
I've been trying not to notice up till now
But I can't escape the feeling
That something's going down now
It's almost like there's someone else around

Even though you're with me
Might as well be by myself
'cause the way you look at me is like
You're SEEING SOMEONE ELSE
The way you look at me is like
You're SEEING SOMEONE ELSE

You can see the same rhythmic strategy in both Verses. I will scan the first Verse.

> I feel some changes in the air
> You haven't been yourself
> You been lookin' kinda dreamy off in space
> Could it be the smell of perfume
> That's starting up this aching
> Or the secrets I see lighting up your face

The 3-stress second phrase becomes more and more important as you get through the two verses.

The rhythm of the Transitional Bridge picks up the 3-stress rhythm immediately, although it is not stated smoothly:

> Even though you're with me
> Might as well be by myself

As you saw earlier, it smooths out for the first time at the HOOK.

> The way you look at me is like
> YOU'RE SEEING SOMEONE ELSE

This strategy works just as well for HOOKS with irregular rhythms. Just put the irregular rhythm in a strategic position so you will have to match it to balance the system. What if your HOOK is

> LAST NIGHT'S LOVE

You could do this:

$$/ \smile / \smile / \smile /$$
$$\rightarrow \quad / \ / \ / \quad \leftarrow$$
$$/ \smile / \smile / \smile / \ldots$$

Now write an unmatching last phrase to unbalance, YET CLOSE the section. Like

$$/ \smile \smile / \smile /$$

or even the very regular phrase,

$$/ \smile / \smile /$$

Because the regular phrase withholds the match with $/ \ / \ /$, the section unbalances. When you get to the HOOK in the Chorus,

> LAST NIGHT'S LOVE

it will be like a surprise party. All the lights come on at once.

EXERCISE 43: FOR EACH HOOK BELOW, WRITE A VERSE THAT USES THE HOOK RHYTHM IN A STRATEGIC POSITION.

1. LAST NIGHT'S LOVE

2. MY FIRST LOVE WILL BE MY LAST

3. THE LAST OF THE LONELY HEARTS

So there they are, five strategies for making your HOOK your hero, basking in the structural spotlight *you created for it.*

1. Put the HOOK at the beginning or end of its section, maybe both.
2. Keep your structure moving forward until you get to the HOOK
3. Repeat the HOOK
4. Use sound to spotlight your HOOK.
5. Use the HOOK's rhythm in other strategic places.

Remember these strategies and try them out. They aren't so hard, and they get even easier with practice. Putting your HOOK in the right place at the right time with the right stuff doesn't have to be an accident. You just need to learn to work the switches.

EXERCISE 44: USING ALL FIVE STRATEGIES, WRITE A SONG SYSTEM FOR THE HOOK "DON'T GIVE UP."

AFTERWORD

If you have worked through this book, you have a solid handle on lyric structure. You know how to make it work for you to deliver your ideas better.

Two important areas remain. One is rhyme: how to find it and use it effectively. The other is lyric content: how to brainstorm ideas and develop them. These are both subjects for other books.